TOTAL CONFIDENCE EVERYDAY

30 REVELATIONS for BOLD CONFIDENCE

JOHN NDEERE

TOTAL CONFIDENCE EVERYDAY

Copyright :copyright: 2021 by John Ndeere

London, United Kingdom

jn@jn.ke

All scripture quotations used herein are obtained from various versions of the Bible. No part of this book publication may be reproduced, stored in a retrieval system or transmitted in any way by any means, electronic, mechanical, photocopy, recording or otherwise without the prior permission of the copyright owner except as provided by copyright law.

Published in 2021 by Jubilee Publishers

admin@jahmene.org

London,

United Kingdom`

FOREWORD

The subject matter of this book presents us with an almost impossible position - one of total confidence.

Is it really possible to walk in total confidence? Is this a fallacy or wishful thinking? By the time you finish reading this book, it will be absolutely clear that yes indeed! And yes you can! Yes you should but most importantly, yes you should begin the journey right away! But we must be ready to walk and to work the process of confidence. The road is available but we must be prepared to walk the journey. The profit is possible but we must invest in the business both at the physical and spiritual level.

When God fabricated and knit you together in your mother's womb, He had absolute confidence in you and endowed you with ability to be the best of what He wanted you to become. But no sooner had you come out into this cold and unforgiving world than that position was challenged and continues to be challenged.

Things beyond your control became reasons for people and situations to undermine your God-given confidence. For instance: your gender may have dictated how you were treated, your family background, reputation or the lack of it, being rich or poor, your race, religion and the list is endless. All these would subtly thereafter have an impact on your confidence. And till today you are still trying to reconcile the deficit.

What really is this confidence? In general terms, and with my years of world class experience as a business leader, I would say that it is being sure of yourself and your abilities. Knowing who you are is truly the authentic genesis of what you can really do and what you can really become.

How many times have you found yourself not sure of yourself and your abilities? Many, many times would be my answer. Yet, on the outside, decked in our nice clothes and beautiful countenance, we may appear all gathered up and well put together, especially when confidence is based on the fleeting material things. If the vanity of life is allowed to define our permanent confidence - where you were born, your beauty, your material possessions, your networks or even on yourself, then we are in big trouble.

My experience is that, it is not until you know who you truly are and make peace with it that you begin to walk in real-time confidence: the genuine and the bona fide level of self-confidence. At that level it ceases to be about what people say or think about you and it also stops being about what you think about yourself. The case is settled when you begin to accept what God thinks and says about you.

When you finally arrive at the place where you define yourself as God perceives you, you walk into an immeasurable state of inner peace and love for yourself. With this you are able to see everything else from an 'outside of you' perspective. You can for example, manage to go through a financial crisis or a relational breakdown and still come out okay. And this is because you know you have the ability to come out of it and build the success yet again. Failure becomes a temporal thing: an event and not a person. After all, a righteous man may fall seven times but He rises up eight. Such is the attitude and the mindset of a confident person who has located their place in God.

In this book, John takes you into a fearless self-discovery journey that makes you see where you are on your journey to confidence. He walks the path with you and doesn't leave until you truly see, discover and confirm your confidence. A confidence that thereafter cannot be easily shaken.

Those who know me can attest that I believe that the physical and the spiritual must meet for total transformation to be realized. Indeed, this is the approach of this book. We believe that God is the centre of our confidence. He is the radar and the bearing from whom the compass of our destiny reads direction. Our belief in Him assures us that we can do all things through Christ who strengthens us. We know that with God nothing is impossible. But even then, we must do what we must, to make this reality a manifest reality in our lives. I am persuaded that faith is not a testimony; the manifestation of faith is the testimony.

So let us agree here and now; we all want to walk this journey and we are not resting until we conquer this mountain and get to the top of it. We shall scale it and subdue it! This is doable and it shall be done for you!

As we read through this book, may the Lord give us this mountain! The self-confidence mountain!

DR ESTHER MUCHEMI:
CEO SAMCHI GROUP

ENDORSEMENTS

1. Reading this book has made me realise how wrong I was about confidence. I am now awake to the fact that I can never be confident in my own strength. However, when I invite the Holy Spirit, He takes away my insufficiency and fills me up with his strength, ability, anointing and truth. My confidence is not in believing in myself, but in Him and His abilities, and in allowing all this to be manifested through me.

2. What really changed my life while reading this book is the practise of being in charge of my emotions, atmosphere and Environment. I didn't know I could create my own reality and dwell in it. I now confidently live by this. I prophecy power and success over myself. It has become a mantra for me.

3. I'm grateful to have had confidence taught to me in such a simple yet very practical manner, while still in my twenties. All the exercises challenged me to abandon the old mind sets and embrace the more liberating ones. I will keep this wisdom as a tool in my arsenal as I soldier on to achieve all that God has planned for me. My life can never be the same again.

PREFACE

We all need confidence! Yes; even the most macho of us. Every person you know of, be they presidents, billionaires, teachers, preachers, parents, managers, your child or your parent, or your next door neighbour; everyone is operating at a confidence level that can be improved. Regardless of our individual measure, we all have a perceived personal deficit that lingers and nags deep down the abyss of our souls. We may wear designer couture, drive Bentleys and associate with the crème de la crème of the 'tribe', but none of us has exclusivity to flawlessness of confidence. There shall always be a silent wish, a quiet thirst and a covert hope for more confidence.

If you are stumbling and struggling with stumpy or dwindling self confidence, you are not alone. Take a deep breath and relax. We are many. I have also been afflicted with the nauseous and pugnacious stench of low self confidence. And came out, or at least permit me to say, I have ingested a worthy dose of self worth to tell the story and have earned the right to perhaps bring out with me some hostages.

Lack of self confidence is bad! It is devastating! It is nasty! It is vicious! It is sadistic brutality packaged in a ferocious packet. I don't mean to praise it but to be brutally honest, no one deserves to suffer the ravages of low self esteem. But before we can walk into the terrain of audacious confidence, it is crucial that we all agree we need confidence. And not just a pea size, but tonnes of it. If we will ever amount to anything laudable, we all need the touch of the great physician and His healing in the area of our self confidence.

I have observed that when you begin to walk the confidence journey, it begins to dawn on you that the question is not how much confidence you have but rather, how much of it you could have. The world begins to bend backwards to you in ways that are simply miraculous. I believe that improving confidence brings many options into play. And the presence of options, and our ability to exploit them, is what makes us prosperous and happy. Each day we are not confident, we significantly bow ourselves to incompetent. Yes, confidence and competence are cousins.

It is one thing to know and experience low self worth but an entirely different story to grow into self confidence. Once your self-value is stretched into confidence it is an experience that you may never want to retract. The idea of being freed from the entanglements of victimhood and loser-ness is one whose impact is incomparable. Imagine living your life everyday without feeling tiny and unseen. Imagine how different your life would be in the absence of that suffocating aura that makes you feel useless and invisible. That is what confidence does: it gives you permission to exist, to speak, to be heard and to call the shots. Self-confidence is faith in your difference. It makes people notice your worth, pay attention and listen to your contribution. And it is what installs us as the CEO's of our lives.

The good news is self-confidence can be attained. It can be obtained. And it can become ours to own. In the words of Barrie Davenport: "Low self-confidence isn't a life sentence. Self-confidence can be learned, practiced, and mastered just like any other skill. Once you master it, everything in your life will change for the better." There is possibility that your life can be permanently changed by an upgrade in your self confidence.

I assent, that self-belief is learnable. It is not a thing out of reach. Self-confidence is not always inborn, sometimes it has to be grown and developed. As a matter of fact, you were not born with things you could or couldn't do: it is life's experiences that subtly taught you to fear and to limit yourself. And for every one of us in whom confidence has to purposely be grown, it takes a deliberate choice of courage not to die in the land of normalcy where fear, intimidation and trepidation want to paralyze you. We have to rise up together and re-learn confidence. Fear has to be instructed to sit down and stop talking.

When confidence is permitted to sit in its rightful throne and rule, freedom finds its fullest expression. And when freedom is at play, fear ceases its tantrums. Confidence is about our ability to know our areas of freedoms, educating ourselves on what accrues to us therein and living out our entire freedom without holding back. God has set us free. He who He sets free is free indeed! He has set our gifts, talents and potential free! But without confidence, that freedom cannot be unleashed into fruitfulness. Without a complete understanding of what that freedom means we may be richly endowed with earth-transforming secrets but continue to wallow in internal slavery of the mind, of the emotion, of the will and of the spirit. Your self confidence is a complete game-changer in the equation of your success.

To be confident is in reality a personal favour we do to ourselves. It is ascertaining that we have acquired the power to exercise the liberty and the freedom that Christ's sacrifice purchased for us. A clear understanding of this allows us to strike the balance between two things: self-belief and self-worship. In self-worship, people overate themselves and over shoot their abilities with superiority complexes, but in self-confidence they believe they can be, they can do and they can have whatever it takes to win, fully aware of their shortcomings and weaknesses. Self-confidence is actually proof that you fully believe in who God made you, yet not in denial of the fact that you are not perfect in all ways. Self-confident people stand on top of their weakness to dare confront challenges with an audacious faith.

It takes more faith to stand up and confront life while deep inside you have had to command fear to sit down and shut up, than it takes by arrogance and pride. I don't want you to be proud. I don't want you to hide behind smoke screens and facades in an attempt to hide your low self worth. I want to teach you how to be confident in the face of sceptics and pessimists. Self-confidence requires that you settle it in your heart that no one owes you anything and that everything you desire shall come to you on the arms of confronting situations, conquering challenges, overcoming personal anxiety, dismantling the damaging undertones of haters, rebuffing rotten opinions of doubters, believing that you can do it, settling in your heart that you deserve the best and forcefully gaining ground because you dared! What people think about you, doesn't have to be what you think about yourself.

I am aware that we all crave to be accepted, to be recognized and to be applauded. We all desire to live in harmony with our loved ones. We live for the day somebody will recognize our efforts and praise us for something. When this is missing or is withdrawn we suffer dejection and rejection.

The withdrawal of love feels like the withdrawal of endorsement. This is because love works hand in hand with our identity; to strengthen it and vice versa. When we are loved, confidence is built because love has affirmed and confirmed what is true about ourselves. When somebody else recognizes us, it strengthens our convictions about ourselves, even though we already knew it before. Appreciation helps us build the courage to do and to be what life requires of us. But what happens if we never get the opportunity to experience this support system? Does that mean we die in the land of insignificance? Absolutely not!

There has to be another way for us to stilt our gait. We have to find another method of scaffolding the construction of our personality. We cannot faint just because people are threatened by our existence. We cannot stop living because people want our strength not to exist. Our confidence is not and should never be up for discussion. It is ours to have and to keep. And those around us, who claim to love us, must train themselves to live with that reality and make peace with our confidence.

This is my underlying conclusion to this matter: when you display confidence, people that are used to a 'sissy' you may get a bit jittery and edgy but you don't live your life to perform for or measure up to anyone's classification of you. Keep at it and soon, their frowns and disapproval rates will become converted from biased opinions of critics to diehard claps of fans. When people fight you because you are confident, it is a silent cry from their hearts betraying their own lack of self-worth. Your most worthy response should be to keep your confidence levels high until you infect them with a good dose of the same. As they re-learn, retrain them to honour you. Confidence is contagious and so is lack of it.

Dont negotiate your worth with people. That argument never ends with your true worth being endorsed; it ends with you satisfying their definition of a weak you. And the moment this happens, you sink lower in and move further away from discovering your true confidence location. You are not a success imposter: you are a bonafide success owner! Dont live your life looking for reasons why you dont belong; discover why you are here! People who dont know your value will have to learn to live with you; not the other way round.

Confidence looks like courage, sounds like leadership, and feels like peace.
- Christy Wright

Your power is not in the hands of another person; stop allocating it to others. Your confidence is not determined by the affirmations of others; it is one decision away from you. It is your prerogative. Your respect is not to be negotiated for; it is to be demanded for through a complete knowledge of who you are.

Grant yourself the same kindness you give others. Endorse yourself in better measures and quantities than you do anybody else. Offer yourself the same, if not better, levels of attention, dedication, loyalty and love that you give away to others. Don't be a slave to impressing people while mistreating yourself. You do not know the estimate of love that you should give others if you haven't given it to yourself first. You are required to love your neighbour as you love yourself.

Confidence is your turning point. It will determine if you will ever make the decision to cross over from poverty to riches. From sickness to health. From weakness to strength. From bottom to top. And from beneath to above! Without confidence you are doomed! But by it, you can re-write your story from scratch and have the ending that you choose. Confidence grants you the permit to live life in your own terms.

From today, receive the impetus to challenge the status quo. Be assured of your power over change. May the confidence that God supplies deliver you to a new day even through you have no experience of that new day yet. Confidence will pull your dominion from the future where it is hiding and bring it to today - and to right now! I have written this book to encourage you to have confidence and put it to work. Employ it and deploy it!

This book is your daily companion to help you on a daily basis to achieve this goal! Read it, sing it, recite it and quote it until confidence becomes one with you! As you read it, again and again, permit yourself to walk out on pessimism and regain your place of authority. Confess the words, the prayers, the meditations and the scriptures here until the power of self-belief is awakened and finds expression in and through you. Each day when you walk out into the ring, the most important thing is your confidence. Guard it. Protect it. It is your ticket to the trophy. Each morning recite God's awesome creed of self-confidence: *"I can do all things through Christ that strengthens me!" outstanding*

I wrote this book because I see your struggle. I hear your silent cries. I perceive the private battles with confidence limitations. I have felt frustration and shame – the shame of low self worth too. I know the taste of it and I want to participate in your solution. Its an honor to. God is with you and He is for you. Believe it and quit living life alone. His grace is for your advantage and His love is for your confidence! He has full confidence in you and so do I.

I love you!

Pastor John Ndeere

Table of Contents

LESSON ONE: WE ALL SUFFER CONFIDENCE DEFICIT!................................... 1

LESSON TWO: CONFIDENCE CAPITAL 7

LESSON THREE: EMBRACE BABY STEPS.. 11

LESSON FOUR: VICTORY BEGINS IN YOUR MIND... 17

LESSON FIVE: DO YOU KNOW WHO YOU ARE?... 21

LESSON SIX: HAVE COURAGE!.. 25

LESSON SEVEN: TEAR DOWN LIMITATIONS! 31

LESSON EIGHT: WHAT DO YOU GOSSIP ABOUT YOURSELF TO YOURSELF? 37

LESSON NINE: CREATE AND CARRY GOOD MEMORIES WITH YOU........... 43

LESSON TEN: WHAT'S YOUR SELF OPINION?... 49

LESSON ELEVEN: WE ARE NOT BLAMING ANYONE AGAIN! 55

LESSON TWELVE: BUILDING CONFIDENCE IS WORK!................................. 61

LESSON THIRTEEN: ARE YOU PRIVATE? 67

LESSON FOURTEEN: MAKE PEACE WITH THE BEAUTIFUL AND THE UGLY. .. 71

LESSON FIFTEEN: PRACTICE HOW TO FACE TENSION................................. 75

LESSON SIXTEEN: IF YOU HAVE TO TAKE SIDES, SIDE WITH YOURSELF, NOT WITH YOUR EGO 79

LESSON SEVENTEEN: MAXIMIZING OPPORTUNITIES 85

LESSON EIGHTEEN: NON-VERBAL LANGUAGE OF CONFIDENCE 91

LESSON NINETEEN: DO YOU CONSIDER YOURSELF WORTHY? 95

LESSON TWENTY: WHAT STOLE YOUR CONFIDENCE? 101

LESSON TWENTY ONE: YOU AND YOUR PROBLEM ARE TWO DIFFERENT THINGS 107

LESSON TWENTY TWO: WHERE IN LIFE DO YOU RANK YOURSELF IN YOUR MIND? 113

LESSON TWENTY THREE: WHAT ECO-SYSTEM HAVE YOU CREATED FOR YOUR SUCCESS? 119

LESSON TWENTY FOUR: HAVE SELF-COMPASSION 125

LESSON TWENTY FIVE: DON'T EXPECT PEOPLE TO KNOW YOU IF YOU DON'T KNOW YOURSELF 131

LESSON TWENTY SIX: DO YOU RADIATE CONFIDENCE OR TIMIDITY? 137

LESSON TWENTY SEVEN: WHAT LEVEL OF MENTAL RESILIENCE DO YOU POSSESS? 145

LESSON TWENTY EIGHT: THE PROCESS OF BECOMING CONFIDENT 151

LESSON TWENTY NINE: CONFIDENCE IS ABOUT IDENTIFYING AND BUILDING OUR ADVANTAGE 163

LESSON THIRTY: WHAT HAVE YOU BELIEVED ABOUT YOURSELF? 173

NOTES AND REFERENCES 181

LESSON ONE

WE ALL SUFFER CONFIDENCE DEFICIT!

We all need confidence! Everyone is operating at a confidence threshold that is insufficient – literally everyone! Less than 1% of people have (accidentally or deliberately) learned how to not experience lack of confidence. Everyone desires to better themselves in this area in one way or another. Regardless of our individual measure, we all have a personal deficit – be it perceived or real. If you are struggling with confidence, you are not alone. Billions of people out there are wishing everyday that they could present themselves more convincingly and invincibly to investors, to employees, to parents, to their spouse, to employers, to the opposite sex, to their opponents, to competitors and to stand indomitable to life in general.

The desire to dominate is an intrinsic parameter in all of us. We all crave to be unbeatable, unconquerable, unshakeable, impregnable, indestructible and matchless, yet an inescapable smoke of vulnerability keeps swirling around us - assailing and accosting us somehow. Threatening to drag us down and keep us from apprehending life, success and prosperity of any kind. We all have moments, persons, situations or habits that trigger, generate, propagate or beget a disenfranchising aura around us. Whether we realize it or not, decertifying or invalidating our own poise is something that a great majority of us are unable to escape.

The lack of a sustainable and quantifiable self esteem is not a unique problem to you - even though it may more often than not feel that way. It may often isolate you and target you, but everyone feels that way at one time or another. People have an inexhaustible list of reasons why they lack confidence. Some feel too white or too black, too thin or too fat, too tall or too short. People of all pay grades, ages, complexions, accents, demographics, Intelligent Quotient and Emotional Quotient are victims of low self confidence. Beautiful girls , handsome men, rich folk and the beggar living under a bridge – each of these people has a legitimate reason for their lack of confidence.

Low self image may isolate you and make you feel exposed and alone, but the reality is that all of us battle this susceptibility. We may appear courageous, defiant or even macho; but there are times, seasons, scenarios or environments that reduce us to jelly. Lack of confidence can leave you feeling terrified in the belly – with a vinegary feeling as though a cinder block is being dragged across the pit of your stomach. Confidence or the lack of it feels like the comparison of the roar of a wild lion – the king of the jungle, in contrast with that of a zoo lion. Both can roar, but anyone can notice the difference. Anyone can see the deficit. And anyone can feel the inadequacy of one with reference to the other. And it is a horrendous feeling!

The question is not how much confidence you have or don't have but rather, how much confidence you could have. In the forest of emotional instability caused by lack of confidence, how can your gait remain unbowed? This is what serves as the beginning of the investment you need to make towards building your confident presence.

Improving your confidence brings many options into play. And the presence of options in life, and our ability to utilize them, is what makes us prosperous and happy. Prosperity in any area is about the options at our disposal – the strings we can pull at a moment's notice.

Bearing in mind that many, many people around us are plagued, even paralyzed by lack of self confidence, it is important to not criticize ourselves too harshly for the lack of self confidence. I share and hold in high regard, the advice of one of the best cognitive neuroscientist and mentor **Dr. Caroline Leaf** – *"Confidence is essentially your ability to handle vulnerability and your ability to handle unpredictable and uncertain feedback and emotions from others"*.

We may not have control over what happens around us. But we certainly have control over how we react to it. This control that we have can be developed, nurtured, grown and processed to the point where we can remain in charge no matter the sudden shifts in our external environments. If you have lost your confidence due to a traumatic event or events – abuse, frustration, broken heart or by any other way – one of the surest ways of regaining your gait is by speaking yourself back into the position of power. Whenever you speak the reality you want to see, you may not see it immediately, but you have made an announcement to your mind that change is coming. A broken confidence doesn't have to be the concretized conclusion of your personality; speak yourself back into the game.

Meditation

Today, identify your confidence deficit. Where do you feel vulnerable? What dis-empowers you? Who demoralizes you? What situations make you sweat? Which situations make you feel targeted? Which doors have you been unable to walk through? What have you procrastinated? Why? What genuine personal reasons do you have (other than excuses)? What deters you? What discourages you? what disuades you? What disenchants you? What hinders you? Who mocks your efforts? Whose presence deflates your morale? What turns you off?

On the other hand: Who is your number one cheer leader? Which words build your resolve? Which scripture gathers you together? Whose encouragement is worth a million dollars to you? Whose joy inspires you to achieve anything? What drives you out of discouragement? Which music or sounds inspire your productivity? Where is your creativity most alive? Write down your answers. They are great pointers to this new journey. Begin living in the environments that repair, resurrect, rekindle and supply fresh confidence. Relentlessly pursue that!

Inspiration

"... Write this. Write what you see. Write it out in big block letters so that it can be read on the run." When you write down and read the vision of your confidence out loud, you demonstrate your resolve to only permit environments that feed your inspiration. Only spend time in places where you are most inspired!

LESSON TWO

CONFIDENCE CAPITAL

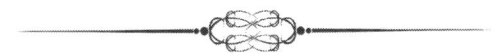

We all have some form of confidence capital. We are not bankrupt. No matter how low we have fallen, how terrible our misery and how devastating our abuse has been, our tank is not completely empty. We have somewhere we can begin from and we have something we can work with. We not only have to believe this truth but we have to accept it and act on it. If you are still alive, that's the only indication I need to prove to you that you can build again – even if you feel like the construction is bound to begin from scratch, perhaps from negative and even from empty. It may genuinely feel like you have sunk so low you have to jump to touch the bottom: but rock bottom is one of the most solid foundations from where to build a sky scrapper. You are not empty: you have just the right amount of capital to jumpstart your confidence journey!

To say the least, I know how the intense pangs of self doubt and the accompanying torment of feeling invisible can damage our persona. When we're stuck in the rut and drained by the agony of self-doubt, it's sometimes very difficult to fathom that there can even be a way out. It feels easier to believe the voice in your head speaking doom and gloom: prophesying that there is never going to be an end or even a quieting down of the loud speaker announcement of low self worth. It feels much easier to blend in, to be common and average like everybody else - to accept fate and stop fighting for difference. But the worst of it is when we imagine the possibility that this is simply never going to go away. If nothing else does, this sinking feeling should be the foremost proof that low self worth is not our natural setting. We were created to be bold! To be courageous! To be confident! And to exercise indomitable all-round dominion!

I am sure the contrast between the expectation and the deficit you feel makes my point clearer. My goal is not to emphasize the deficit, but to bring your faith to focus on the spark of hope that has remained. We don't need much; just a spark is enough to light the fire. The little left is enough to build your confidence from a cup to a reservoir. And from a bucket to a lake.

Confidence can give birth to more of its kind. Confidence trains your mind to dwell on possibilities until they stop being a far away pie in the sky; unique only to a select few and become your new normal way of thinking; your new way of perception. Confidence really does bring miracles within reach!

Today focus on possibilities! Disallow that sinking feeling of inadequacy, that confidence shortage, and that 'emotional defectiveness' feeling. Begin from the confidence you have to build the confidence you need. Do what you can, then do something new. Begin to step outside of your comfort zone, until your confidence territory becomes enlarged. See possibilities, believe in miracles, try new things and become relentless at courting new frontiers. Schedule your pleasures because pain always schedules itself.

Confidence begins with a decision! Now that you know you are at a deficit, make the decision to experience a different reality. Imagine how different life can and shall be when you row in confidence. Now begin aggressively and decisiveness to move towards that new reality.

Meditation

Today, consider what you have. Visualize it. See it. Search it out and look for it till you locate it. It's there, even if you don't believe it. We cannot move forward until we answer the question: "What do you have in your hand?" in the words of the Master – "The simple truth is that if you had a mere kernel of faith, a poppy seed, say, you would tell this mountain,

'Move!' and it would move. There is nothing you wouldn't be able to tackle."

Locate your mustard seed size of confidence and the seed shall soon become a tree. And in that tree we shall grow a forest!

Inspiration

"We're all adrift in the same boat: too few days, too many troubles. We spring up like wildflowers in the desert and then wilt, transient as the shadow of a cloud. For a tree there is always hope. Chop it down and it still has a chance - its roots can put out fresh sprouts. Even if its roots are old and gnarled, its stump long dormant, at the first whiff of water it comes to life, buds and grows like a sapling."

LESSON THREE

EMBRACE BABY STEPS.

It is vitally important that we don't give up on our confidence growth. Regardless of the battles we have faced, the possible continued emotional injuries we may be incurring and the demeaning scenarios we are likely to encounter along the way; we mustn't give up on confidence. The truth of the matter is that there are things we will never access if we give up on this journey now. Our families, friends, children, colleagues and we ourselves deserve a significantly confident version of us! In this new version lie a better future, a stronger life and a victorious existence for all people around us. This battle is worth every punch!

Regained or new found confidence can restore our life from

previous loss and set us on a pathway to permanent recoveries and discoveries. It is possible to live an unstoppable life! With the right tools, strategies and scriptural techniques you can build a confidence mindset! You don't have to live life at the pity of events, victimized by happenings and persecuted by life's occurrences. You don't have to live life enduring missed opportunities, unfulfilled potential, and drowning in regrets. You don't have to feel less-than-enough one more day! The wisdom of confidence can change you today; and right now! The power of God's confidence can restore what was lost and reverse what was done. Believe this and begin the journey of change!

To commence this significant transformation, we must of necessity make a conscious choice to walk out of the past – in all its forms, shapes, sizes, tastes, memories and moments. Making this decision is probably one of the smartest moves you will ever make. However terrifying it may feel, leave the past in the past!

The past however loud can make no promise! The past however ugly cannot threaten the dream God put in you! The past with its history cannot change God's prophecy over your tomorrow. The past with its stereotype narrative cannot stop the miracles lined up for you! The past and all your haters in it cannot stop the reviving hand of God in your life! The moment you decide to move into a brand new day – a brand new dream and as fresh start, things will begin to line up to support your decision. Begin to make emotional investments in your future through compelling dreams, vision and imagination. See yourself confident, bold and courageous. Imagine the future you and direct all your passion towards making that dream a reality.

Permit me to remind you this important truth: God has not deposited your victory in the past: don't look for it there! He put it in your future: focus there! No matter how loud the regrets and the guilt of the past can shout, they will never outdo the voice of a made up mind. Don't look back; you are not headed that way. Look forward; that's where greatness eagerly awaits you. Look up; that's where life is cheering you on! And look ahead: that's where you are headed.

Remind yourself constantly that you are scheduled for successive successes. Verbally declare over yourself that the rest of your life shall be the best of your life. The moment you begin to focus all your energy in your future, it will suddenly dawn on you that it's too late for you to fail!

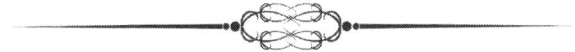

Meditation

Today, consider where you lost your confidence, and where you didn't gain it as you should have. Whenever you find yourself fallen in life, don't look for the place where you fell; look for the place where you stumbled. A person, an event or a situation gave birth to your current low self worth. There is a thief that broke through your walls – a snake that desired to bite you. Look for that moment that your security perimeter was breached.

What makes you stuck in self-doubt and short of confidence? Despite your accomplishments, what is that thing that makes you feel like a scam destined to be exposed? What makes you feel that you don't deserve unconditional and fulfilling love? What breeds rejection in you? Why do you feel like people who genuinely love you are just pretending and they are too good to be true?

Other than the 'introvert excuse' what makes you scared to meet new people, why do you prefer to stay home feeling you have nothing to offer people? What is that thing that makes you feel ugly, stupid, overweight, too dark, too tall, boring, never good enough or constantly guilty?

Trace the traumas, the failure, the source of rejection, the anxiety, expose the negative beliefs and identify toxicity and criticism from loved ones in the present or the past. Admit where you have had skewed beliefs or unrealistic expectations that resulted in emotional wounds in you. Lack of confidence is not natural: it is caused by something. If we can identify the root of the disease, we can treat the malady!

Armed with this information, make the decision to confront the unique set of challenges that have made you into what you have become. Accept what you cannot change – but first locate the cause. Change what you can but understand it before you attempt to change it. From this position, begin to disallow stumpy self confidence. Declare an end to all present low self value and embrace a brand new bold life! Everything begins with a decision - everything!

Inspiration

There is a power in you and behind you helping you to achieve anything you put your mind to. This power makes your efforts to be like seeds thrown on a field by a man who then goes to bed and forgets about it. The seeds sprout and grow—he has no idea how it happens. The earth does it all without his help: first a green stem of grass, then a bud, then the ripened grain. When the grain is fully formed, he reaps—harvest time!

If you will plant the little confidence you have into this journey, you will be surprised at how your new mindset will transform your entire world. When you know the truth, you can never go back to a lie. When you set yourself to pursue freedom then you will experience for yourselves the truth, and the truth will free you."

"The mind, once stretched by a new idea, never returns to its original dimensions."

— **Ralph Waldo Emerson**

LESSON FOUR

VICTORY BEGINS IN YOUR MIND

Your mind and your brain constitute a miracle! They are the hardware and the software that make you infinitely capable! While your confidence depends on this supernatural architecture in a natural setting, your insecurity and self doubt set foot in you through suggestions of limiting thoughts planted in your mind over time. To be restored to the miracle of confidence as God intended, we have to unlearn these limiting concepts, ideologies and subtle lies. Furthermore, we need to guard against a relapse into self doubt by relentlessly building a fervent personality, a vibrant soul, a gallant mind and the charisma of spirit deliberately!

Building confidence is hard work. That is the truth. It takes tough choices, daily commitment and a deliberate effort to break old habits of fear and retrogressive self image and begin building a new one of power! It is an easy choice to resign to fate and just fit in. But when you understand how crucial your confidence is to your success, the risk of indifference becomes too expensive for you.

Not everybody embraces the concept of hard work. Most people expect magical solutions and miraculous divine intervention in things they should be taking pride in changing. It is not only fulfilling but greatly rewarding to build your tattered self confidence from the ground up with your own hands. But the story of that success does not begin with actions and behavioural modification: it begins with a change of mind!

God will not do miracles for you every day. He will not intervene in everything. He will not do what is up to you to do. He doesn't replace you: He empowers you to do what He instructs.

Confidence is best built on the move – in action! But before you move and before you build, you must make that crucial decision. Decide that you are going to be confident. Make up your mind that you belong to the confidence club. Your decision will unlock the miracle of audacity! And when you are audacious life has to submit to your reign.

Meditation

Today, watch your thoughts. Frisk them in search of lies and any disempowering suggestions. Scan them till you expose all the agents of low self worth. Forbid negative talk around you and stay away from toxicity of any kind. Only allow thoughts and conversations of power, of love and of a sound mind! Only permit an atmosphere of confidence, integrity and power to thrive around you. Disallow weak conversations, avoid guilt laced talk and excuse yourself from accusatory undertones. Conversations that pull other people down end up pulling you down. Thoughts that lift other people up end up lifting you up too.

Inspiration

Summing it all up, friends, I'd say you'll do best by filling your minds and meditating on things true, noble, reputable, authentic, compelling, gracious—the best, not the worst; the beautiful, not the ugly; things to praise, not things to curse. Put into practice what you learned, what you heard and saw and realized. Do that, and God, who makes everything work together, will work you into His most excellent harmonies.

LESSON FIVE

DO YOU KNOW WHO YOU ARE?

A great part of your confidence comes from knowing who you are. Do you know who you really are? Do you understand the power at your disposal? Do you know your capabilities, capacities, gifts, strengths and unique identity? There is incredible power in aligning your thoughts, actions and choices with your core identity and purpose.

Your personal brand has an influence, it has a following, it has a fan base and it has a reward system! When you know who you are, what you are not will stop talking. It is impossible to walk in the confidence of a champion when your life's roadmap is based on a model that you don't own, let alone understand. There is a miraculous dimension of confidence that is birthed when you line up all your aspirations, dreams, desires, prayers and action plans with your core being.

Countless people live a fake life. Each morning they wear a facade to help them fit in to a world that is real. I cannot begin to even pt an estimate to the number of people who are social chameleons – changing colour to disappear into their environments because they have no compelling identity and no persuasive personal brand that they are proud to present. The system of things in which the world runs has no helped to curb this situation. Each morning people who have ignored their confidence wake up to serve the dreams of the very few who know themselves.

Lack of confidence affects people of all walks of life; but that is not an excuse to be its victim. It affects CEO's as well as paupers; but that is not a reason to submit to it. It controls the young as well as the old; but that should not be a permit to grow old in low self esteem. The most deceiving aspect of it that I have observed is that most people who are making a reasonable income assume that they are living at their personal best. Income does not equal potential. And money is not a measure of personal value. Achievement is fleeting: here today and gone tomorrow, but emotional stamina is a far more non-transitory achievement. If I had a chance to make money or to understand my potential better for a season, I would choose the latter. Potential cannot be quantified. And understanding who you are is the gateway to unlocking an immeasurable amount of confidence capital.

Do you know who you are? Do you truly know your value? Do you understand your difference? Do you comprehend your worth? I am not talking about your pay grade (that is somebody else's opinion of you): I am talking about the latently dormant supernatural power invested in you for an outstandingly astounding outcome. When you know who you are, confidence will begin flowing like an unquenchable river. And when you are confident, the world will begin to salute your efforts and honour your presence with awards and rewards.

Meditation

Today, understand that we are 'human beings' and not 'human doings!' our power flows from what we are before it flows from what we do. From now on, be proudly you: people will adjust! Make them learn to accept and live with the version of you that works for you! You once lost yourself: never lose yourself again!

Inspiration

Since, then, we do not have the excuse of ignorance, everything—and I do mean everything—connected with that old way of life has to go. It's rotten through and through. Get rid of it! And then take on an entirely new way of life—a God-fashioned life, a life renewed from the inside and working itself into your conduct as God accurately reproduces his character in you.

LESSON SIX

HAVE COURAGE!

A lot of changes in your life are not gonna take a mere wish, desire or talk: it will take courage – a load of it. A lot of people know what is good, what is right and expedient but the courage to do what is right and expedient is not in everybody. Wisdom is amazing. But wisdom without strength has no power. This is where the difference begins.

It takes courage to desire to reveal the real you! The thought of revealing yourself and facing rejection or repercussion of any kind is not encouraging. That is why courage and confidence go hand in hand. Confidence peels back the layers of devious lies and limitations that trying to work hard for acceptance and for love, subtly built in you over the years. There is a version of you that a courageous confidence is yet to reintroduce to you. That version is worth every work, every sacrifice, every investment, every effort and everything you have got.

Regardless of your age or the societal standing that your life has solidified around, living a lie one more day is not different from being sneaky and sly. Take time to tenaciously unlearn insecurity tendencies, overcome setbacks, overlook disadvantages, overpower insufficiency lies and give yourself a second, a third, a fourth and a hundredth chance if that is what it takes. Take the adventurous journey of finding out who you would be if you were not forced into who you currently are. Confidence will turn you into a brand new person - a person that you will have to reintroduce to people.

Courage means that you begin to prophesy to your day every morning and call it what you want it to be. Pronounce blessing, profits, breakthroughs, favour, beauty and advancement. Regardless of how it unfolds, let your words of hope, faith and courage precede your plans, actions and goals. Your day is as good as you chose to see it. Today is a good day! Yesterday is history and tomorrow is a mystery. You're just left with today. Why not start the day on a good note and notice everything good about this present day. Enjoy today to the fullest and learn to put a close to events in your life as soon as you possibly can. Good ones and bad ones alike. Don't wallow in the bad or linger in the good. Don't reel in the pits and in the mud, and don't dwell on glory and in the pomp. The secret to achieving ground quickly is in moving on swiftly.

Search for truth and bond with it. In all your becoming, become truth! Build yourself with and in truth! Remember that reputation is not what makes a man, it is integrity and honor. Reputation can be sacrificed for a bigger goal; in other words, popularity can be postponed, until vision becomes a reality. Don't be caught up in what others think they know of you; be concerned with what you know about you. Take time to soul search and adjust every place you have a low opinion of yourself. Find out what caused that level of perception and adjust it quickly. Make alterations that make you enjoy more of the life you have per time instead of trying to change your world to make it better for you. "You have to change your thinking if you desire to have a future different from your present."
- Germany Kent

Furthermore, don't be obligated or always driven by protocol, rules and compliance. That should not be the first and foremost consideration in making your life's progress. Don't be a slave of routines and traditions so as to please people at the expense of your heart. To think inside the box is to be subject to the box. Consider stepping out of it and thinking who you truly can become outside of the prejudices of stereotype opinions. We are not made for the rules of life; the rules of life are made for us. Think well of yourself and dictate how your life should turn out. It is within your prerogative.

I am excited at the prospect of watching you go through an extreme makeover. If I were to pay for your transformation I would do so without a second thought. I know what it means to be suffocated with a simulated life – trying so hard to achieve things as an undercover human being. Playing along and singing along

– a song that I don't own. It doesn't work. Life is waiting and it is designed to respond to the real you and not your bogus pseudo. Sing your own song! Quit the cover songs! Dream your own dream. Build your own life. Be present in your own life and make things happen. Take a front row seat and tell everybody else to take the rest of the seats. You are the driver: we shall go where you say!

Meditation

Today, take time to think about the things that fear, poverty, desperation and low self esteem has made you do. What you find out could be your history, but it doesn't have to be your destiny. If you will question and interrogate life this way, a new day is about to dawn over you!

You don't belong to coincidence; you belong to an intentional divine plan for significant impact. You belong to an organized, intentional and deliberate strategy to make you count in the mathematics of destiny. You are not an accident or an isolated incidence, somewhere at the corner of the cosmos; you are a huge part in the grand game of life. You matter and you are needed at the table of greatness. To disqualify yourself with small talk and small thoughts is both unfortunate and ignorant. The question is not if the world is going to accommodate you in that plan, but rather, what are you doing in an organized way – deliberately - towards becoming significant at the place where life requires your input.

We need you! We need what you have! This world is incomplete without your confident contribution.

Inspiration

Be fearless! Fearless means taking the first step, even if you don't know where it will take you. it means being driven by a higher purpose, rather than by applause. It means knowing that you reveal your character when you stand apart, than when you stand with the crowd. – Chadwick Boseman

Be strong. Take courage. Don't be intimidated. Don't give them a second thought because God, your God, is striding ahead of you. He's right there with you. He won't let you down; he won't leave you.

LESSON SEVEN

TEAR DOWN LIMITATIONS!

Confidence is about being able to function without being immobilised by mental limitations. A lot of our limiting and negative thinking can be traced to bad company, a damaging memory or a painful experience. Despite the fact that each one of us has had to pass through these scenarios, all of us have picked up varying degrees of emotional disability. Whether we know it or not, we have attracted limiting beliefs, toxic mentalities and cunningly damaging habits. This is why it is paramount to learn to take a step back and do an audit of your life every so often – to pinpoint limitation-thinking.

A limit can be referenced to mean one or more of several things.

It can be a limiting condition; restrictive weakness; perceived lack of capacity; imaginary inability or fantasy handicap. But mostly, limitations exist in the mind. This is because breaking limits has subconsciously been associated with breaking rules. Although rules keep us safe, they also keep us predictable and that by itself can be a limitation. Life and success is about the ability to break barriers, overcome predictable patterns and curve a niche for ourselves beyond and above established patterns of performance. Boundaries, limitations and restrictions can be good and bad at the same time. The question is how you interact with them to your advantage.

Breaking limitation requires faith. Bold faith! Your faith frames your world. That means, whatever needs to manifest in the practical, tangible, spendable and physical scene is mandated to do so by your faith. Without faith, we exist in the abstract and the inconclusive white elephants of life. Your believe forms the framework within which limitation is broken. When faith creates realities, fallacies and propaganda fall off. Furthermore, you receive not what you deserve, but what you are expecting, as informed by faith. Your faith is an actively creative agent that forces deception and limitation to sit down and keep quiet.

To inform and build your faith is a foremost strategy in changing your realities and your experiences. Faith is not a mere escape tool from life's challenges or for the soothing of your soul through life's tribulations; it is a force that converts intangible things into tangible consumables. In other words, faith is the axe that cuts asunder the limitations of life. It chops off doubts. It extinguishes the lingering smoke of self doubt.

To put this better, think of a printed photo that is not framed versus one that is framed. If I throw the unframed photo at you, it is not a threat and neither does it pose any danger. It will probably be blown away by wind as soon as it leaves my hand. But if I throw the framed one at you, you will be ducking for cover. That is what faith does to your dreams. It gives them frame, form, structure and solidity. It makes them noticeable, effectual and accommodate-able! It gives solidity to your life, your ideas, your values and your identity. Faith converts dreams into real estate!

Faith therefore is the stair case out of the prisons that life has jailed us in and separated us from possibilities; including low self confidence. It is faith that demands that you de-categorize and de-compartmentalize yourself from all preconceived notions of what you can or cannot do. You see, to do or to be is first a concept in the mind, followed by a confession in the mouth. There is nothing you do before first saying in your mouth or in your heart. This declaration of intention is where the action happens. We don't perform tasks when we complete them but when we declare our intentions to do them. Everything including eating, buying, walking - everything we do - is first an intention, a silent or loud declaration, then an action.

That means that our manifestation is a carbon copy of our intentions. And this revealed intention betrays our mentality. That means that our final outcomes and incomes are a proof of how we have categorized ourselves and compartmentalized our worth into notions, beliefs, classes, cliques, clubs: all of which are informed by doubts about ourselves. Faith is the place where you break the limits of your life. Think and speak of yourself as able to do all things. The person that says they can and the one that say they cannot, are both right.

At this place called faith, you have to rewrite your mantra, your vision and mission. You have to re-narrate your capabilities to yourself. Make yourself into a person that you can respect. Re-create yourself into a person you can honour, fall in love with and pay a premium to listen to. If you are unable to do this for yourself, find somebody that can introduce you to yourself afresh. You see, we have to see ourselves from the supernatural ability to be and to do anything we set our minds on. But if we don't know our abilities and capabilities, we constantly become subservient to limited potential. Ignorance is the root of many problems.

We have to spend time to understand ourselves - the inherent powers, the resident capacities, the possible stretching and the bearable demands we can possibly accommodate. If you were a car, ask yourself this: are you utilizing all of your manufacturer's installed horsepower? If you are underperforming, don't blame the maker. Service your engine and 'vroom', 'vrooomm' and 'vroooooommmm' out of every limitation!

Draw a strategic life plan. Don't consult past failures, current drawbacks or the opinion of visionless and sightless folk. Everything that stands, drives or flies began as a plan. From a car, a plane, a building, an investment or a piece of equipment. If you have a desire to walk, to run or to fly - a plan is your first consideration. It's not a negotiable factor if to draft a detailed and systematic plan to move your life forward. You have to do it.

Life is not what the years deliver but what the minutes and the hours demand. Design your minutes, your hours and your days.

Learn how to leverage wisdom, vision, information, relationships, property and money - swiftly. The difference between the rich and the poor, the successful and the failed, is swift decision making. Decision making is a fundamental x-factor in the success equation!

Life is lived once and life, like they say, is not a rehearsal. To live below your potential is a de-service to self. To exist only and not to live abundantly is a waste of time and divine opportunity. Live life to the full live life on your own terms! You deserve every perfect, full, whole and best of everything! I believe limitation can be broken. It should be. It ought to be. And it must be! Broken!

Meditation

If confidence will have a chance, the decision to lock out limiting external forces that dilute it has to be taken. When God is about to bless you in a mega measure, He first makes your circle smaller. And when He sets out to do this for you, it is paramount that you comply. There are people, weaknesses and situations that adulterate your power and infiltrate your personal control over life. They have introduced and continue to fund limitation agendas in your life. Recover yourself from such things and such people. Recuperate from compromise, guilt, mediocrity, fear and bad company. But more importantly, stop the self sabotage of feeding a fixed mindset that says you cannot change, or it is too late to change. You don't have to live a second rate life: resolutely get back your full confidence! The entirety of it!

Today tell everyone and everything that sells limitation to you that you want a refund!

Inspiration

God can do anything —far more than you could ever imagine or guess or request in your wildest dreams! He does it not by pushing us around but by working within us, his Spirit deeply and gently within us.

LESSON EIGHT

WHAT DO YOU GOSSIP ABOUT YOURSELF TO YOURSELF?

Self confidence is not arrogance or pride; it is first and foremost learning how to speak to yourself, for yourself and about yourself. Self-talk builds self-belief and how you see yourself becomes how people see you. All confidence flows from self-perception. The secret is not to work on your habits of security but on your self-concept.

Your words are powerful! They are the agents that create your world; experiences and realities. Words are also the agents that reveal the world you have created for yourself. Without your words, we don't really know you. It is not the dictionary that gives meaning to words: it is your heart. Words are powerful; take them seriously. Words can be your salvation. Words can also be your damnation.

Spoken words carry a potency to form, to transform or to conform. The words we speak or the words we hear are not consonants and alphabetical sounds; they are creative forces and energies that can cause things to happen, to crystallize or to materialize. Further to that, even the thoughts we think create waves of power around us.

Our subconscious mind is somewhat a very interesting space. When we speak anything, it first applies it to us. That means that when we say bad things to or about other people, our subconscious assumes that the first recipient of those words is us. That's why we feel bad after throwing careless words at people or feel wonderful after speaking good words to people. And this does not merely affect humans, but it also affects nature. This sounds farfetched but it is factual and proven.

Dr Emoto, a Japanese scientist has researched extensively about this phenomena. In one of his experiments he observed that speaking positive words to a sample of water resulted in the water's crystals forming beautiful geometric shapes whereas speaking negative words to another sample from the same water resulted in the crystals smashing and forming destructive shapes. This is a verifiable fact that is in the public domain.

All of creation with all its grandeur is solely a product of words. How then can we ignore the creative power of words over ourselves? Armed with this knowledge, it is fundamentally important to design your life with your words. Yes, you can design your life - bespoke! Custom made! Tailor made and custom-built.

Our tongue is a bulldozer. It can *wreak havoc* or it can build sky scrapers. Self talk is desperately crucial in the weaving of the fabric of our self confidence. We have to vet, interrogate, frisk and sieve the words we speak or hear. In fact we must practice selective hearing and selective speech. The tongue in your mouth is as a bit in a horse's mouth that controls the direction of an entire horse. It is as a rudder in a ship; small but of great consequence. The words that are uttered or heard are powerful enough to bring about life or death to anything whether a person, plant or situation. Your confidence is irretrievably dependent on what you speak and what you hear.

Words are soldiers that can be sent into battle to war and conquer the world around us. Send them to repair what is broken and to build what has been torn down. Send them into your future to create the family, the wealth, the health and the situations that you want for yourself! Use your words to reconstitute and reconstruct the atmosphere for your confidence. You thrive in atmospheres you create. Use your words to construct these environments actively and proactively.

The state of affairs at hand may not match your confessions yet but confess anyway. Those around you may not understand your reasons for doing so but do so anyway. Do not shy away from making grand confessions about your future because you are afraid of what people may think. Their thoughts count nothing in making your destiny beautiful. They have no clue how much battle you have had to face to get here. Ignore their scepticism and pessimism and build with words. Do not speak reality, speak faith!

Superintend over your life until your situations catch up with your revelation!

Our words are a reflection of our heart - out of the abundance of the heart the mouth speaks. Inform your words by the meditations of your heart. Let your heart and mind be full of good things – occupy them with things true, noble, reputable, authentic, compelling, gracious—the best, not the worst; the beautiful, not the ugly; things to praise, not things to curse. Put into practice this wisdom and God, who makes everything work together for our good, will work you into his most excellent harmonies.

Meditation

Today, use your words to create an environment that feeds your self-value and shun all avenues that cast doubt on your worth. Stay away from people and situations that second guess your abilities and those that tarnish your reputation, colour, capabilities and competences! Say and believe things like - I am intelligent, I am respectable, I am honest, I am excellent, I am preferred, I am favored, I am a solution giver! When I show up, grace, love and wisdom arrive! Gaining and maintaining your confidence is not an easy task but it is doable especially if you can purge your environment and sanitize your mental and emotional space.

Today, remember who you are, what you are capable of and what you outdo everyone else at. Do not allow life to make you forget your power and your authority. Remember that you are the best you that there is. You are the only version of you in the entire universe! Stand up and make your contribution!

Inspiration

"Because God gave you your makeup and superintended every moment of your past, including all the hardship, pain, and struggles, He wants to use your words in a unique manner. No one else can speak through your vocal cords, and, equally important, no one else has your story." (Charles R. Swindoll)

LESSON NINE

CREATE AND CARRY GOOD MEMORIES WITH YOU.

Building confidence involves recalling and narrating past conquests, victories and testimonies to yourself. This creates a compelling reminder that you are bigger than your present doubts, shortfalls or imaginary inadequacies. Remind yourself that you have overcome defeat, failure, sickness, being maligned, bias, mourning, distress, depression, hatred, joblessness, mental breakdown, malice, false accusation, jealous friends, envious relatives and impossible episodes of life's tests to get to where you are right now. If you are alive, you have a story to tell! That story is not a narration of how life conquered you but of how you arose from its attempt to disfigure you and came back to tell the story! If you are reeling from a shaken gait or a wounded composure, your confidence has not been lost; it has only been momentarily hidden by the clouds of today's rain!

Life has a way of making good times seem to last very briefly while painful seasons seem to go on and on and on. In fact, because of our negative nature, life is subconsciously interpreted like a week; 'five working days' but only 'two-days-weekend'. Life can and should be one long 7 days weekend. It can be a party if we want it to. But it can also be torment if we make it one.

Every day, every single human being alive is faced with certain diverse chances and a sure myriad of opportunities to be sad, anxious, weak or angry. In fact, the default setting of life in our mind is arguably disappointment. We first sense the negative before we recognize the positive. We unconsciously first realize the bad in a situation and react to it rather than respond to the good in it. Negativity may come so naturally to us that we don't even realize our lens is distorted. For many people negativity is as natural as breathing. They don't think about it. It just happens—and they certainly don't question it.

In psychology negative bias is our tendency not only to register negative stimuli more readily but also to dwell on these events. This positive-negative asymmetry means that we feel the hurt of a reprimand more strongly than we feel the pleasure of praise. It makes bad first impressions more difficult to conquer and makes past traumas to linger for a long time. In almost any interaction, we are more likely to notice negative things and later remember them more vividly.

However, happiness is not the absence of pain or regret; it is a perception that chooses to pick the good available right now no matter the insurmountable bad at hand. It is the ability to pin point the advantage in every disadvantage including the worst of experiences and the mental 'toothpick' that can pick a grain of good from a bowl of misfortune. The basic truth is this: You cannot have a negative mind and experience a positive life, it is impossible!

Mind shift is a daily meal to happy people. In fact, instantaneous disposition adjustment is the adaptability requirement for champions. My most compelling reason for writing this book is to help you step out of normal living and become an everyday champion. I want you to win per hour and per minute. And mental discipline is one area i highly recommend that you master.

It is a precious thing to master the art of identifying the good in everything. Turning down the opportunity to be upset is a grand step towards happiness. The grand rule is this: worry, anxiety and ingratitude about past good, will steal the ability to enjoy let alone identify present good. No matter how bad things get, never forget they once were good and there is nothing new under the sun, they will become good again! No pain is permanent and no problem is an end in itself. There is no misfortune that is absolute or pain that is pure. In every mess, there is good. Sometimes take stock of the places God has taken you to, the dangers He rescued you from, the advantages He gave you over others: count your blessings, name them one by one. By the time you are done, you will be apologizing for complaining about the bad in your life. Don't be quick to forget good times. They will become the fuel you need during bad times. Document your testimonies. Remember the stealth, the silent and the 'under-cover' miracles that happened to you. Appreciate the preservation, the opportunities, the chances and the favours you received along the way. Remember the friends, the support and the love of family that God has allowed you to enjoy. Disallow present inconvenience from clouding your judgement. Live in the positive, in the pure hope and in the authentic belief that all things shall work together for your good in the end no matter how ugly the look in the beginning.

If in this life you become nothing else, please become a prisoner of hope and a hopeless optimist at that. You could be in mourning, but you have not always mourned, remember life and be glad about that!

When your mouth is about to outpour with legitimate, justifiable and logical complains, don't utter a word, and fill it instead with recitations and memoirs of good times. Choose to hold a 'positive and upbeat view of the past'. Accustom your tongue to speak well no matter the reality and experiences accosting you right now and no matter how long that pain may have lingered. The facts about your present pain do not negate the truth about your past joy and the possibility of future recoveries.

Find the good in the bad and sing about it. Look for it, till you locate it! Your life is not only made up of bricks of pain, it also has blocks of good, fun, advantage and happiness. Those too are part of you. Look for them, re-member them; add them back to you! No matter where life has fixed you, find the fun in it, look for the joke in the duress and locate a smile in the midst of it all. Smile! You look so much better when you smile! Don't get angry at problems; solve your problem without becoming one. There are many ways of killing a rat without burning the house!

Meditation

Confidence has a lot to do with your emotional intelligence. How we manage our temperaments and how we adjust to adapt emotionally is vital in shaping our confidence. I believe we can be happy. We ought to be happy. But joy is called into our lives. It is not an automatic emotional disposition. Preserving an atmosphere of self confidence will demand the remembrance of precious moments of success, greatness, victory and laughter. It will mandate the conscious creation of an aura of joy and a canvas of gratitude to light up your world. Remember the good times and recall joy back into your life.

Today, go on a search mission, locate every good thing that happened to you, see every advantage you received, identify every miracle that came your way, and rejoice over everything that went well, all that happened right and the opportunity to even have been alive to see it. Don't face life angry, discontented and with a sense of irrevocable entitlement. When bad comes, don't reject and fight it, accept, move on and shout back at life with a gracious and courageous proclamation; "bring it on!" Life is not an ATM where only good things must be withdrawn, sometimes, life can give you a negative account balance but that's not the end of 'banking'. Deficits are never permanent!

Today when you see the clouds obstructing the sun, be patient.

Shake yourself from the ashes and dust yourself up! The sun will shine again! Wait for it. Remember not so long ago, you enjoyed the sun. God is in all things working for your good. If it is not yet good, it is not the end. If it is not yet good; He is still working. Give Him time!

Inspiration

Once again I'll go over what GOD has done, lay out on the table the ancient wonders; I'll ponder all the things you've accomplished,and give a long, loving look at your acts.

LESSON TEN

WHAT'S YOUR SELF OPINION?

"*A man cannot be comfortable without his own approval.*" Let those words first simmer. Let them sink before we settle down and say anything else!

The opinion of you begins with you. Nobody is to blame for your bad name, bad reputation or the low goodwill associated with your name. You are both the marketing manager and the public relations department of your life. You set the tone of respect for yourself before anybody else picks the cue. The temperature of honour, the ambience of admiration and the quality of attitude with which people conduct themselves around you has a lot to do with how you have trained them. Your self-opinion is the table of content that we refer to before we can impress and imprint our chapters in your life.

Further to that, what you radiate also subtly influences people around you to conduct themselves in a certain way. Your spirit has an effect; an undeniable influence that your countenance exudes. Whenever your soul is weak or dysfunctional, or when your spirit has been broken by whatever thing, it shows on your face. When people read this, they unconsciously label you with victim or prey labels. But when you have invested in your confidence, joy, power and mental aptitudes, people readily submit themselves to your influence. They can't help but listen, follow, obey and salute.

Confidence is about respecting yourself enough to want to be you! It is admiring yourself enough to want to be around you! Confidence is about getting out of your own way and allowing your God given prowess-to-subdue-life to come into effect and do its work without interference. You function best from within a calm, kind and deep love for yourself - love and not arrogance!

What we think of ourselves has cannot be trivialised. It has a lasting ramification on us. In the words of Norman Vincent Peale your thoughts create you world - "change your thoughts and you change your world." We become what we constantly think and there is no escaping this reality. Our thoughts are the ingredients that determine what we become. And what we become determines what we attract.

Who we are becoming is playing a mega role in what we are attracting. If we want good things, we have to build ourselves up in confidence, skill and excellence through the thoughts we permit to inhabit our mind. Unfortunately we rarely know how to give ourselves permission to think highly of ourselves.

On the contrary, we readily permit the opinions of others, their insecurities and their weaknesses to become the eyes through which we see ourselves too. We assume that we are more or less like our average friends and therefore we deserve to be labelled with their categorization.

I have come to learn a very important lesson on my journey of life. That God is not a respecter of persons! He doesn't categorize us into personalities that should or should not be blessed, healed, honoured or ignored. With Him there is no class, clique or club of people that are special or preferred. Anyone can activate the blessing over themselves and the blessing shall respond equally to any and to all! The disqualification does not happen on God's table: it happens in people's minds about themselves.

My question is - how deserving of the best life do you consider yourself?

Who have you decided should be blessed before you?

Who told you that you are second class?

When you imagine riches and honour, who comes into your mind?

If it's not you, why?

Meditation

Today, get out of your way and let your inbuilt power of confidence drive you. Recover your confidence of innocence by reversing the effects of learned fear and acquired insecurity. Call out these vices for what they are. Through self confession and faith in God, outdo the impact of failure and cumulative moments of self doubts - whether imposed by others or self inflicted. Pray until God heals your wounds of low self worth and helps you embrace the totality of your original confidence settings.

Today, admire yourself. Identify the traits that make you awesome, celebrate them, and thank God for them. God invested in you an amount of confidence that your entire life cannot exhaust. Search it! Recall it! Regain it! Ignite it! Run it! And be it! Be confident again!

Begin working on your self-concept! Vote for yourself! Endorse yourself! Expect the best in your life!

Don't backdate or postpone your miracles!

You deserve them today!

Don't push blessings to others! They are yours too! Accept them! Take them! Have them! Keep them!

If you will believe that God wants the best for you, the best will begin to want you!

Inspiration

"Don't be afraid, I've redeemed you. I've called your name.

You're mine. When you're in over your head, I'll be there with you. When you're in rough waters, you will not go down. When you're between a rock and a hard place, it won't be a dead end—Because I am God, your personal God,

LESSON ELEVEN

WE ARE NOT BLAMING ANYONE AGAIN!

Life can sometimes become overwhelming, even to the point of a standstill. In technology we say, it can 'hang'. When the moving parts of life become clogged and the thinking patterns or software become rusted, motion can be hindered and progress hampered. Each one of us at one point or another has become paralysed by fear, pain, loss or misfortune. In like manner as a gadget, to press the reset button becomes the only option for life to shake up and jumpstart. Reset means to adjust again after an initial failure or to set back to the initial state of function. Regardless of the cause of the congestion or redundancy, several things can help unlock the quagmire and get us back on track – bringing with it both a refreshing and a flourishing. Taking responsibility is one such reset button.

Success takes extreme ownership. By this I mean, the ability to accept and own your good times and the bad ones alike. This means that if the future must retain its brightness for you, you of necessity must say no to excuses. Extreme ownership demand that it's in 'ME' that 'WE' succeed. Blame game is not part of the success tournament. Don't blame your leader, your colleague or your junior. You participated in the failure! And you ought to participate if not to initiate the corrective measures to reset things and restore the success trajectory. The reset journey begins with this question - what was my part in creating the problem?

Failure to take personal responsibility is a sign of a bigger problem. It points to your inability to lead yourself through life. If you're not actively and freely taking responsibility for your life and what happens in it, it's almost certain that you're blaming other people or situations for your misfortunes. The ridiculous thing about the people who you target with blame is they probably don't care about how you feel, or they have no idea anyway. And they don't have to, because your life is not about them. It's about you.

Failure to take responsibility may be a pointer to a low self value. People who have low self esteem generally don't take responsibility for their lives. They don't have the capacity to view themselves as any worse than they already feel. They instead accuse other people. Self-esteem won't be boosted until you wise up and take responsibility. Until you stand up to yourself. And until you call yourself out for bullying your future with the tantrums of yester-days. Responsibility sanctions you to take action to improve yourself and your environment.

Responsibility and blame are inescapable. They have to be apportioned every day: to somebody or to something. It works like an unspoken rule of life. But playing the victim card can lead into an irretrievably broken life. Toying around with the illusory advantage of preaching victimhood and justification for life's unsatisfactory conditions erects a gloom atmosphere in your own life.

Victimhood is a bottomless pit that never gets satisfied with anything. Whether it's deadbeat relationships, a bad childhood experience, poverty, rejection, or other inevitable hardships like loss of a loved one – or any situations that inevitably come with life, it's always something other than yourself that's at fault. Playing victim is falling prey. Don't do it.

The mentality of finger-pointing is a very dangerous type of self-stagnating, self-sabotaging belief system. It doesn't just undercut the individual but undercuts the wider society around him as it insatiably pursues self comfort, self righteousness, self justification and all other 'selfs' available. If all is to blame but you, the entire picture of a viable solution is not yet in the picture. We don't have control over the world we live in; but we have control over ourselves in the world. If we can change us, we have changed our world already.

Furthermore, taking responsibility and taking the blame are two different things. If you take responsibility, nobody has to take the blame. Taking responsibility is the closure that shuts down the need for blame. When you judge yourself, you cannot be judged. As a law of life's justice, two judgements for the same crime is tantamount to injustice. Life apportions blame where nobody has taken responsibility.

Don't blame anyone or anything: we empower the person or the thing we blame. When we discover our confidence deficiency, we are likely to believe that we are that way because we are flawed, insufficient or inadequate. We tend to think that we missed something or are disadvantaged in more ways than other people. We may blame others, blame generational curses or habits and what people did or didn't do for us. This entire mindset is built on a lie!

The truth is that we were not born insecure, we simply forgot and buried the version of us that is incredible, naturally talented, supernaturally gifted and the side of us that is unaware of limitations. We lost it through bad teaching, awful programming and stifling social conditioning that left us believing that we are less than the best. Whether we did this consciously or not, we participated in the process that made us this.

We must be ready to 'own' what we 'cause' if we truly are honest and sincere. The truth is, if we honestly want a better situation, how bad the current one is will become irrelevant as we relentlessly pursue the change. What you don't confront, chances are, more often than not, you will never conquer. So, there has to either be a choice to live with mediocrity and protect an ego or to sacrifice 'feel nice' and 'look good' selfishness for excellence.

my suggestion is this: what if you knew that taking responsibility of your low self esteem would set you on the right path towards confidence recovery: would that inspire you to do it? I am not at all suggesting that you assume blame for the molestation, abuse or violence that robbed you of your confidence, but standing up to whatever or whoever caused it and declaring self leadership out of it!

Question where you are! Be comfortable to ask and be asked tough questions. A question is a gateway into solutions. In fact, a question unlocks doors, opportunities and seasons. The status quo remains until a question challenges it. Oppression persists until a question breaks it. Poverty continues until it is questioned. Low self belief persists until it is stopped! And life remains at the level of what is available until a question reveals what is possible. The power of a question cannot be underestimated if we truly desire our lives to change. Self-confrontation requires that we be okay to interrogate ourselves and investigate every stubborn thing and every person that has resisted our progress.

Meditation

Today admit your wrongs and take responsibility of your errors. Often times we are stuck because of ego and carrying around the burden of a ‹big head›. To reset your life takes much more than vision, it takes humility. And being humble is not a weakness but a strength. You are wholly or partially responsible for where you are. And whether somebody or something else caused your current mess, the responsibility of fixing what is affecting your life is squarely yours. To accept liability is the proof of maturity and the initial step towards creating a better future outcome. Holding onto the past is a sign of victim mentality and blaming others for what happened is a sign of pride. If failure happened, it was an event. And failure is not a person: therefore you are not a failure.

Today, consider that you deserve to live the life you dream of. You deserve to know how to convert dreams into reality. You can create success on demand! You can summon confidence on demand. God can grant you an on-time anointing to influence life's moments. This anointing called confidence determines the certainty to succeed! Create, own and protect a plan to get you back to this original position of power, authority and emotional control!

"An important decision I made was to resist playing the Blame Game. The day I realized that I am in charge of how I will approach problems in my life, that things will turn out better or worse because of me and nobody else, that was the day I knew I would be a happier and healthier person. And that was the day I knew I could truly build a life that matters." – Steve Goodier

Inspiration

Let all bitterness, and wrath, and anger, and clamour, and evil speaking, be put away from you, with all malice: And be ye kind one to another, tender hearted, forgiving one another, even as God for Christ's sake hath forgiven you.

LESSON TWELVE

BUILDING CONFIDENCE IS WORK!

We either live on the path to greatness or wishing we could. This is the reality of every human alive regardless of their status in society, pay grade, beauty, country, skin colour or gender. We all want to better ourselves, move forward and make progress. Nobody plans to remain in one spot all their life. We all want to be wanted, and desire to be desired. Everyone wants to be loved and appreciated. However, the propensity with which we want change in our lives varies from person to person.

How badly do you want to be confident? How intensely do you admire the people that live their lives on their own terms? For how long do you want to tolerate a life of meagreness, just-enough and dreamlessness. For how long will a purpose-driven life escape you? These questions ought to give you sleepless nights. At least in my estimate, these questions should provoke, even irritate you until you begin a journey to build your life into something you are proud to look at.

Confidence is about gradually breaking forth from the restricted circle of potential that most people live in. Limits are real but they should not be our prison. This continuous process does not happen overnight – it is not an occurrence or an event; it's a habit. Confidence helps us safely break the imaginary rules and boundaries that our subconscious mind has created. It is in itself a personal prison break!

Confidence is about being certain of your abilities and stretching them to the maximum at any given moment. It is about applying yourself one hundred percent in every moment you live. It is not only a feeling that things will go well but also an accurate judgment and optimism based on correct self assessment that things will work out, and then engaging on the journey to make that a reality!

Anything we set ourselves to learn becomes a frontier in which we can potentially break forth with power. Persistent effort, relentless pursuit and commitment to apprehend recovery must remain at the crosshairs of our focus. If you quit on the process, you are quitting on the results. Success is a slow but rewarding process. Quitting does not speed it up; it postpones it. Each day should be an opportunity to raise the low place of your life back to honour, power and respect.

Write down where you are and where you want to go.

Confidence requires a clear communication of dreams and expectations. Expectation is inversely proportional to frustration. Uncommunicated expectations breed unspoken frustration. The world of vagueness and guesswork is where suspicion and resentment dwell. Success does not thrive in generality: it abides in specificity. As long as its path is defined and refined, results have no choice but to manifest. Maybe your frustration with the people that have broken your confidence is because of uncommunicated expectations. Write down what you want, what you desire and what you expect from those around you. Communicate it with precision and attach deadlines to it. Whatever has been defined can be achieved. And if achievement is not happening, then definition is wanting.

At other times, I have encountered situations where the problem is not with somebody or something else but with me. Sometimes, a state of limbo persists because of an elephant in the room. An elephant is anything or anyone that cannot be questioned. Elephants start small but they grow big! Very big! And the only way to deal with them is to be comfortable enough to have awkward conversations. If you don›t like awkward conversations your life will struggle. Needless to say, it›s easier to move an elephant when it›s small. The prudence of addressing matters at the budding stage inside your heart cannot be overemphasized. Elephants in the room have caused the collapse of homes, companies, churches and even nations. Elephants may, especially when young, look nice and funny but soon, they grow bigger than the room. The sad part is that sometimes the elephant in the room is you! Deal with it!

How have you participated in the defeat you are currently in? What was your role in the loss of your home, the deficit of your profits or the stagnation of your life. Whose life have you messed up and which person have you failed? Whose heart have you broken and which person have you taken advantage of? Reset is about fixing what is broken, mending what is torn, renewing what is old, healing what is sick, refunding what was lost and a fresh start for all concerned. Walk to them and apologize. Send back what you took. You may not recover what was lost but you can mitigate further loss, stop heartaches and redeem life. Do the right thing!

Repentance is a powerful place to rebuild confidence. When the haemorrhage of confidence is stopped, power returns. When guilt stops bleeding life, confidence begins to win! And the victory that confidence brings is the kind you will never again allow to be stolen.

Meditation

Today, build your confidence. Invest in your smile, joy, power, respect, honour and glory. Don't study your shyness, study what gives you boldness. Don't study your weakness; study your strength. Don't study what makes you common; study what makes you different! Forget what people expect of you; build until you redefine what they should expect of you. Put into practice what makes you light up a room when you walk in. Build what makes you outshine your peers and embarrass your naysayers. Build what gives you a cutting edge, an upper hand and a spring board. Rehearse it until it becomes a natural instinct. Begin today; begin right now! Maintain progress relentlessly!

Inspiration

God can do anything — far more than you could ever imagine or guess or request in your wildest dreams! He does it not by pushing us around but by working within us, his Spirit deeply and gently within us

LESSON THIRTEEN

ARE YOU PRIVATE?

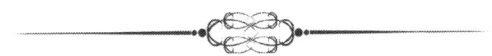

Recently I read a meme that really changed my perspective. It actually annoyed me more than it cracked me up. It said: *"Don't take social media likes too seriously. Most people who like your photo are seated on a toilet seat"*

As a social media expert and having built and led one of the best social media teams in modern times, that statement hit me with a level of truth that I just couldn't deny or ignore. Social media gives me a thrill – especially with the kind of results I have witnessed, but this meme annoyed me because part of my result analysis is in the number of likes a team can garner. But to imagine that they came from somebody seated on a toilet seat somehow deflated my ego. Well, that is the reality regardless of what we may like or not like. Social media is a two headed dragon! A tool for business and a drug for some addicts. A profile builder and a lie at the same time.

There is a destructive trend in most societies that destroys success mercilessly. It is the need to report progress to an imaginary audience. It is on this foundation that social media is founded. We may not readily want to admit it, but perhaps too many minutes or even hours of our day are spent scrolling through feeds as a time waster.

Social media has taken over our lives. It shapes opinions', drives fashion, and advertising. But the worst effect of it is that it has replaced genuine human to human relationships with fake virtual imaginations. Feelings are now emojis and we no longer have a way to verify what is presented. If somebody posts themselves in the business class of an aeroplane, we don't know if he flew business class or he stopped by there to take a photo. As though that is not enough, we now even have photo studios that imitate private jets. What a lie!

We have come to the era of unrealistic standards of success and beauty. We have created this monstrous opportunity of showing only the best and most enviable moments while concealing efforts, struggles, and the merely ordinary aspects of day-to-day life. The pressure is now officially on to look perfect, to impress peers, and to frustrate haters while hiding behind this digital curtain. My greatest concern however is not this imposter syndrome that threatens to reduce our society into a cartoon network, but its ability to create the perfect storm of self-doubt.

Being privy to and associating with uncommonly successful people, I have continually observed a common denominator trait among them: privacy and discretion! One astounding proof of confidence is the ability to succeed in silence – overcoming the need to announce your chessboard moves. Confidence sometimes, does not need expression by words, it requires loud silence. Silence is a tactic of speaking up. Silence negotiates. It centres you and allows you to differentiate between what is urgent from what is important.

An argument is proof that you don't have an explanation. But silence allows us the opportunity to understand the facts at hand and apply wisdom to create an atmosphere of confidence, even in the most hostile scenarios. Silence can wake us up from extremes and provide eloquent answers in our lives. It can give us a gentle nudge when something doesn't feel right by putting us in touch with our intuition. When silence provokes purposeful living, confidence is built. And without silence, emotional regulation and mental clarity is near impossible!

Highly effective people only allow you to see what they have decided to. They are not driven by pressure to report to, compare with or imitate others: they are driven by their private purpose! Their success is more important than fame and to them fame is not synonymous with success.

This ability to remain anonymous and private seals the leakages of personal confidence. It protects integrity robs gossips the opportunity to reduce you to their level. When you know formulas and methods of success that other people do not know, that is what is called power! When you can control outcomes, govern results and direct trends without revealing your secrets; that is called confidence!

People only fight you with the weapons you handed them. Privacy is your defence weapon, use it! Retain your energy and preserve you confidence!

Meditation

Today, keep quiet! The best response to doubters is s i l e n t successive successes! No one argues with results. Prove your confidence in what God has deposited in you by working it out until it works! Every successful person has a secret. Keep people out of your business. Have secrets between you and God. Secrets of power, honour and greatness!

Inspiration

Whoever spreads gossip betrays secrets, but the trustworthy person keeps a confidence.

LESSON FOURTEEN

MAKE PEACE WITH THE BEAUTIFUL AND THE UGLY.

I grew up in abject poverty in my native country Kenya. My family was a happy and complete one with a father, mother and awesome siblings but we were extremely poor. Being a sharp boy in school allowed me to have some pretty daring dreams of one day travelling the world, owning a car and having a happy family of my own. Such dreams were ridiculous to my fellow poor kids but I kept them alive.

Although my childhood was marred with squalor and disadvantage, after performing exceptionally well in my primary education, I got a sponsorship to the best High School in the country then, by my late British mentor Dr. Geoffrey Griffin. This introduced me to a very different world view. At Starehe Boys Centre, I came into contact with the cream of the country – the best of the best boys drawn from all areas of the nation. Here, I also came into contact with exceptionally confident young people whose poise began to rub on me in the right way.

Until I met my age mates who had grown up in well to do homes, with resources and skilled parenting, I didn't know that growing up in hardship would deal such a dent on my self confidence. And though I knew my parents loved me a great deal, the ridicule, shame and the humiliation of poverty had undoubtedly dug a huge hole on my confidence levels. Without a doubt, I can say that confidence is sometimes enhanced by our access to resources that make life better or easier. Whether that access creates exposure, buys hope or lessens the weight of present pain; confidence is strong when resources abound.

Life always serves two things: adversity and advancement. Make peace with that. Life is like a bicycle: today one pedal is up while the other is down. And the next moment, what was up come down and what was down goes up. We may not be privy to the schedule of the two, but we can bet that each will turn out to be so at one point or another. Confidence is about learning to gracefully embracing both in equal measure. Rejoice over the fun when it comes and don't be opposed to tough episodes of life, as and when they come. Acceptance is about taking life as it is – especially what we cannot change.

Avoidance doesn't improve things, it postpones precious moments through which we can learn and grow. Anxiety is amplified when we live in denial. Today I look back to my childhood with reminiscence of pride despite the low moments and meagre supplies. I remember some of my peers who couldn't face the pain of poverty and ended up in drugs, early marriages and illicit liquor. The inability to face tough seasons can be detrimental.

Acceptance is not passive resignation; it is positively acknowledging and working with the resources at our disposal, both inner and outer, to mitigate, heal, redirect, and change what can be changed. Through acceptance we assent to the reality of a situation, recognizing the process or condition, however uncomfortable, without attempting to change it or protest it. It is the awareness of a present moment without judgment. I advocate for radical acceptance – the one that focuses on gratitude in all things. Even when life feels unfair, unexplainable and grossly intimidating, we can retain our confidence and stand our ground.

When we enter rest while in tough situations, we are able to apply our values accordingly and compromises becomes less likely. Faith is not denial of reality: it is acceptance of what is, before it becomes what it can become or what we hope. When we don't accept where we are, a cheaper version of confidence called ego, comes into play. Confidence is the wisdom that interprets life in a realistic language so we know that as we go through it, we grow through it.

Meditation

Today, you may be handling far tougher challenges than i have ever had to face. But allow me to submit to you that there is no new problem under the sun. What is facing you has faced other people and it has been defeated. Every problem has an expiry date: even the one you are in. I believe in miracle: what seem like a forgone case can be turned around in a moment of time. Yes; cancer can be healed. The lost child can return home. The business can come back from losses and make a miraculous comeback. Your set back is a set up for a comeback! If you can submit to God's process gratefully and accept life's progression courageously, it is only a matter of time before confidence is recovered!

Inspiration

Be cheerful no matter what; pray all the time; thank God no matter what happens. This is the way God wants you who belong to Christ Jesus to live.

LESSON FIFTEEN

PRACTICE HOW TO FACE TENSION

Confidence is about the ability to handle tension – the feelings of tightness, overwhelming anxiety, and uncertainty. It is the aptitude to control anxiety and panic in all of its guises - depression and painful low moods, stresses, worries, doubt, anger and frustration.

Emotional tension is the result of living with a badly fitting assembly of our thoughts and feelings – where these two are not reconciled or in agreement. This internal turmoil is often times as a result of how you really want to be being replaced by what you think you should be. Externally, irreconcilable differences between people can bring tension and animosity. And this can greatly eat away our confidence as individuals. You can imagine the kind of damage that an irreconcilable mind, will and emotions can do.

On average, stress causes many people to crumble. Diseases, low immunity, joylessness and low productivity are some of the indicators of this kind of stress. The average person is not able to handle stress positively or at least channel it as fuel for enhanced performance. Confident people are able to thrive in spite of added tension. They remodel stress, pressure and tension into stimulants and energizers. In fact, they view adversity as an opportunity or an asset and not a liability.

While people with weak emotional intelligence struggle to cope with pressure, confident people know how not to descend into victimhood and victim talk. Instead of 'why me?' mental dispositions, they quickly switch into 'if not me who else?' They have this open mindedness that constantly reminds them that challenges are inevitable. We have no control over how life reacts to us each day, but we have the power to drive our will, our emotions and our mind. When anxiety arises, we can dedicate our resources towards doing what we can to keep moving forward.

Confidence keeps problems in proper perspective. No exaggerations and no blowing things out of proportion. Confident people constantly know how to rephrase the feedback generated by their environments into proper language that makes everything non-monstrous. To them, there are no catastrophes; only challenges. There are no fires; only flames. There are no threats; only urgent matters. And there are no dangers; only hazards.

Confident people respond to situations by reframing the memo they give themselves. They refuse to allow gloomy, cynical and unenthusiastic inner monologues to go berserk.

Confidence as an emotional astuteness can help you cope with emotional pain. A lot of people in an attempt to avoid facing challenges fill their to-do-lists with activities. Confident people know how to tone down on the need to feel needed. They instead strike that crucial balance between a healthy social life and alone time, even when they're stressed by one thing or another. In the words of Hermann Hesse, they know that *"Within you, there is a stillness and a sanctuary to which you can retreat at any time and be yourself."*

Confidence means the decision to not run away from uncomfortable situations and conversations – internal and external. During tense circumstances, confidence can bear instant rewards of admiration, love, connection and trust from self and from other people. Being a 'nice' person is not always a good thing. Face confrontations and uncomfortable situations with confidence. Be direct and forthright with yourself and with those around you. Confidence creates a way forward in confusion, allays fears and restores the accurate arrangement of things – order!

Motivation

Today, confidently bring yourself to authentic self-awareness – the person that God created you to be and the life He gave you to live. Handle tension promptly! Don't wish it away – face it! There is no single place in the world of faith and miracles where worry has been granted the power to perform any miracle.

Don't worry! Surround yourself with the harmony of God. And enjoy God kind of outcomes! Don't panic! Fear not! Have faith! Only believe! Even in tension

Inspiration

When you're feeling intense "ugly" emotions it's hard to bring back some control and work through the emotions. One thing I always recommend (and it's not easy but so effective!) is to ask yourself: what can I learn from this? This simple question will make the biggest difference for your mental health and mind! **Dr. Caroline Leaf**

LESSON SIXTEEN

IF YOU HAVE TO TAKE SIDES, SIDE WITH YOURSELF, NOT WITH YOUR EGO

Every human being suffers from negativity bias. This is an inherent trait of leaning towards losses more than opportunities or the tendency to dwell on mistakes instead of successes – on doubt more than on faith and on fear more than courage. It is a natural tendency to be more negative than positive. We can think of this as the asymmetry or the unevenness that we exhibit in our judgement or inclination towards good or bad. 'Negativity Bias' refers to our proclivity to "attend to, learn from, and use negative information far more than positive information" (Vaish et al., 2008, p.383). Not only do negative events and experiences imprint more quickly, but they also linger longer than *positive ones according to researcher Randy Larsen, PhD,*

This inclination is a precautionary logic that flows from our ego. Our ego is that part of us that 'purports' to protect us from any sudden change from the norm. The ego wants us to live in a safe zone with no threats or any need for abrupt adjustments. In a bid to keep itself relevant, the ego chooses to rather be negative and then slowly work towards equilibrium than be positive and risk being disappointed. According to Freud psychoanalytic theory, the ego seeks pleasure (i.e., tension reduction) and avoids pain, it is concerned with devising a realistic strategy to obtain pleasure. The ego has no concept of right or wrong; something is good simply if it achieves its end of satisfying without causing harm to itself.

According to Freud's personality theory (1923), *the ego ideally works by reason. It operates according to the reality principle, working out realistic ways of satisfying the demands of life, often compromising or postponing satisfaction to avoid negative consequences of society. The ego considers social realities and norms, etiquette and rules in deciding how to behave. The destructive part is this: If the ego fails in its attempt to use the reality principle, and anxiety is experienced, unconscious defence mechanisms are employed, to help ward off unpleasant feelings (i.e., anxiety) or make good things feel better for the individual.*

This is where confidence comes in. Confidence confronts ego. It stands up in the face of danger and reminds us that the best cause of action is not to cower and hide, but to face it and conquer. Confidence is about the courage to swiftly face and neutralize the counterparts of ego - these thoughts, emotions, notions, imaginations and anxieties that push us outside of our zone of peace, joy and thereby edging us out of our productivity.

If not tamed, the ego can ride you like a horse all your life. While you are the stronger one, the fastest one and the mover in the equation; an untamed ego can run you with its little and slow miniature self. It is our confidence, if well developed, that can stand up and lead from the front allowing us the opportunity to face challenges without picking up an excuse or a reason to always look for alternative routes.

On the other hand, it is prudent to remember that confidence does not do well in a toxic environment; it thrives in positive emotions. The good thing is that positive emotions have an out-doing effect on anxiety thereby restoring confidence to its ideal environment within a short moment. But this has to be proactively induced. When negative bias threatens our stability, we need to quickly bring into play our positive emotions of joy, excitement, calmness, peace and serenity. This promptly restores both our confidence and our focus on what is good and beneficial.

I personally would advocate that we retrain ourselves on how to call back our emotional centeredness at will. I enjoy being able to call myself to order at any moment and bringing my soul (my will, mind and emotions) into subjection and order. This is called self-rule. Any inability to reign over our soul threatens all our other things in our lives. Sometimes you may need to pray; calm down, listen to worship music or take a walk; but emotional missiles must be subjugated at all costs. When you are confident, you not only confront and address other people with astute firmness; you also can call yourself to an internal meeting, and tackle your volatile internal members.

If you must take sides; choose your side. Stand up against your ego. Let confidence have the last say. Confidence is the voice of God. Don't hit back; discover beauty in everyone and in yourself. If you've got it in you, get along with everybody. Don't insist on getting even; that's not for you to do. "I'll do the judging," says God. "I'll take care of it."

Motivation

Today, listen to the melodies that calm your nerves. Have a good hearty laugh. Play the sounds that heal your troubled soul. Visit the places that keep you energized and rejuvenated. Avoid toxic people and situations. Forgive quickly and be at peace as much as you can. Give your confidence the food and the drink that it craves.

Inspiration

Dear friend, guard Clear Thinking and Common Sense with your life; don't for a minute lose sight of them. They'll keep your soul alive and well, they'll keep you fit and attractive. You'll travel safely, you'll neither tire nor trip. You'll take afternoon naps without a worry, you'll enjoy a good night's sleep. No need to panic over alarms or surprises, or predictions that doomsday's just around the corner,

Because God will be right there with you; he'll keep you safe and sound.

LESSON SEVENTEEN

MAXIMIZING OPPORTUNITIES

Your ability to succeed on a regular basis has a great contribution to make in your confidence journey. The more you win, the more confident you feel to attempt more ventures, try more opportunities or stretch yourself more to become a better version of yourself. How much more would you apply yourself if you knew that you would win? Confidence is the reason you dare to apply yourself more in any given venture.

There is one builder of confidence that you simply cannot ignore. It's called preparation. When you prepare adequately, you foresee twists and turns before the twists and turns show up. You engage questions before they are asked and provide answers before they are required. Preparation brings you to the game, helps you run the game and win, before opponents, participants and spectators show up. When you are well prepared, people don't show up to the game to watch the match; they come to see you win.

The more prepared you are, the more confident you are to perform at your best. Confidence is about our ability to thrive under pressure and to perform at our peak, while others seem to crumble in similar situations. Confidence is about creating the engine of success using efficient parts such as precise attitude adjustment, accurate mood setting, optimal performance and processing of goals, sufficiently studying and knowing your opponent, it is about mental toughness, dedication, concentration, and focus and the intelligent harnessing of both inspiration and perspiration for the best possible outcomes.

Preparation means the ability to get into 'the challenge state' to enhance our performance and to avoid at all costs 'a threat state' which interferes with our abilities. Do you feel challenged or threatened? This is a question you have to be willing to ask yourself before you enter every opportunity. Threats create fright. Challenges create inspiration. What state are you competing at? How aligned are you with your true self? What worth are you creating in line with your true value? Are you sabotaging your capabilities by ill preparation?

Preparation is also about creating a winning conduciveness or aura - creating the right sights, sounds, feelings, and even smells. It is about creating your most productive daily routing that gets you in rhythm and harmony with your best performance. I value greatly my atmosphere every day. I am constantly choosing what to listen to, whose space I enjoy and whose words add value to my self-worth. I proactively shun toxicity and selectively pick conversations and associations – not with a fork but with a toothpick.

I am cognizant of the fact that confidence requires me to visualize myself in advance, performing well in an upcoming presentation, interview or pitch - over and over again. Visualizing a successful performance instils confidence in my ability to perform at my best. The way I spend my time right before a big performance will influence my chance of success. Whether I am making a presentation, preaching a sermon, counselling somebody, doing a business, writing a book or meeting a new potential associate; i prepare! It's my mandatory ritual.

Today deliberately structure your self-talk. Say to yourself "be strong," "focus on success," and "give everything", Replicate competition conditions during training sessions as much as possible. Train with the same mindset that you want to utilize during competitions. Prepare thoroughly, mentally and physically, so that your confidence levels are high when you compete. Always be in competition mode – home and away, in training and during the game. Train courageously as you would compete. Don't worry about your fears and shortcomings; you have more going for you than against you. Courage is built on action in spite of fear. Build! Action! Prepare! Opportunities come from God, but preparation comes from you. And when opportunity meets preparation success is inevitable!

Meaningful change takes time. But it takes confidence to wait... without confidence, our lives are filled with haphazard, short term, unorganized and scattered efforts. Faith requires a level of stubbornness. It requires you to prepare even when there is no promise of an upcoming game. What has delayed you has not delayed God; your opportunity will come in its time. But when it does, let it find you ready! Opportunity does not come to those who wait; it comes to those who are prepared.

Opportunity is maximized by preparation! Preparation begets confidence and confidence permits wisdom to bear fruit. If you will operate in preparation, confidence in your opportunities will deliver supernatural outcomes.

Motivation.

Today, prepare youself for the future you dream about. Actively begin to organize your mind, your body, your language and your time around the big dreams that sound far-fetched. Without faith and hope, we dont deserve tomorrow. Without action faith is dead. Your preparation is proof that you have faith and hope in the dreams you profess. Prepare even when there is no indication that change is coming. If you prepare, your opportunities will reward you for honoring them when you didnt have a reason to.

Inspiration

... Look at an ant. Watch it closely; let it teach you a thing or two. Nobody has to tell it what to do. All summer it stores up food; at harvest it stockpiles provisions. So how long are you going to laze around doing nothing? How long before you get out of bed?

A nap here, a nap there, a day off here, a day off there, sit back, take it easy—do you know what comes next? Just this: You can look forward to a dirt-poor life, poverty your permanent houseguest!

LESSON EIGHTEEN

NON-VERBAL LANGUAGE OF CONFIDENCE

All communication is both verbal and non verbal. There are things you are saying without saying. There are words you are emitting without opening your mouth. There are statements and utterances you are making with your mouth shut. Your behaviour is saying something. Your countenance is shouting something. Your presence is setting in motion a judgement on you. Confidence or the lack of it can be read without your words being consulted.

Confidence has an observable gait to it. Body language is a physical proof of the presence or the absence of confidence. If well developed, processed and harnessed, it can help you decrease your level of stress, and remain both in control and in charge of your personal space at anytime. What if I told you that you can command attention and drive conversation by summoning your confidence in an instant, would you believe me? This is true and you can achieve it. I have practiced this and won by it, any day – any time.

Confidence drives influence. And effective personal influence depends on our ability to inspire and positively impact people around us. That is why confidence is a game plan that is un-ignorable. At any given instance, people we're hoping to influence subliminally evaluate our credibility, measure our empathy, estimate our self belief and test our trustworthiness using a combination of what we say and the gestures we use to accompany our words. Their judgement *is only* to a degree determined by what we say, but more so by our use of our personal space - our physical gestures, posture, facial expressions, and eye contact.

Whenever our gestures are not in full congruence with our verbal message, people subconsciously perceive fraudulence, duplicity, uncertainty or internal conflict and they begin to 'switch us off'. When we're able to maintain eye contact, we're communicating to others that we're honest, approachable and confident. *"The most important thing in communication is hearing what isn't said."* - Peter Drucker.

According to Carol Kinsey Goman, the author of the book *'STAND OUT: How to Build Your Leadership Presence'*, and a *Leadership Strategy Contributor on Forbes.com*, first impressions are extremely crucial. First impressions are made in less than seven seconds of a physical encounter and are massively influenced by reading our body language. And once someone mentally labels you as "trustworthy" or "suspicious," "powerful" or "submissive," everything else you do will be viewed through that filter. When you meet someone for the first time, they're subconsciously taking a rapid inventory of your gait, your smile, your handshake, and how you present yourself. They're also subconsciously deciding if you're genuinely nice, if they want to know you and even if they want to work with you, all in those first few critical seconds, merely based on what they see, and how you make them feel. Confidence understands that we don't have a second chance to make the first impression.

Confidence is about what we exude. Assertive posture, power poses, and appropriate eye contact decide a lot of the confidence game. A straight back, a confident walk, raised head, looking up instead of down, firm handshake, locking and maintaining eye contact, and gesturing with an open hand, palm facing up, has a positive effect on others. It communicates acceptance, openness, frankness, sincerity, candidness, cooperation and trustworthiness, and is an indication that we don't feel anxious, nervous, or afraid.

People who are not able to maintain eye contact or are the first to break eye contact indicate that they're hiding something, feeling uncomfortable, or projecting a lower-status than or submissiveness to the person they're speaking with. Mike Tyson one of the greatest boxers of all time says he would accurately predict almost all of his matches when he first looked his opponent straight in the eye. If his opponent blinked first, Tyson knew the game was already decided in his favour.

What are you saying about yourself in the environments

you visit? What deposits are you investing in new associations, relationships, business leads and new encounters with new people? Are you conscious that you are creating a perception about yourself each time you show up? But most importantly, do you know that you can drive that impression deliberately and predictably?

Motivation

Today, exude confidence! Clothe your entire self with confidence. Practice smiling – it not only makes you more attractive and trustworthy, it also improves your health, your stress level, and your feelings about yourself. G**ive a firm handshake and** Stop fidgeting. Inspire respect by practicing the confidence body language. Today, remember that the best confidence designer is walking in truth, integrity, being honest and sincere – staying away from guilt and character taint of every kind, as much as you can.

Dont live a safe life: live a life of significance. Put yourself out there packaged in the right packaging material - confidence. Life responds to confident people. You can begin to change your life right now by designing your confidence proactively!

Inspiration

There are no better cosmetics than a severe temperance and purity, modesty and humility, a gracious temper and calmness of spirit; and there is no true beauty without the signatures of these graces in the very countenance. ~ **Arthur Helps**

LESSON NINETEEN

DO YOU CONSIDER YOURSELF WORTHY?

Every human being must ask themselves this one question as early in life as possible: "How do I know *my* worth, and how do I know it before it's too late?"

Self-worth is not how people evaluate and classify you; it is how you value yourself. It's not what others think or don't think about you, what you have achieved or not, the deadlines you have actualised in life or haven't – self value is determined, calculated and set by you for you. I would love to tell you that it is easy to ignore outside forces when it comes to determining your self-worth, but that would be untrue. As a matter of fact, unless we deliberately build this standard, external factors continue to inform us of our worth.

I love Amy Morin's (L.C.S.W., a psychotherapist) perspectives on psychology. On self worth, she explains that whether we know it or not, we constantly measure our worth, but we're often not aware of *how* we do it. We use different yardsticks and benchmarks. Sometimes it's by our career, family, love, body shape, beauty, income or outcome. This however, is a very dangerous method. Its randomness and not its intention is what is somewhat inaccurate. We shouldn't measure our worth based on moving targets or randomly shifting goal posts. If it's with money, how much money is enough to make us feel worthy? What if we get there but our friends have achieved further milestones?

It is unreliable to measure our worth this way. The mathematics is flawed – and deeply so. She continues to say - "When it comes to measuring self-worth, many people use something just as unreliable as a random stick," "You may not even consciously think about what type of stick you use to measure your self-worth. But it's likely that, deep down, you know. After all, when you feel like you're measuring up, you feel good about yourself. But when you feel as though you've fallen short, your self-esteem likely plummets."

The danger is this – the stick we decide to use is often outside our control or influence. We don't own it. And when this is the scenario, our self worth and the stick tend to work against us. **We notice how our sense of self-worth affects us, but we rarely stop and think about how we're doing our calculations.**

The best "measuring stick" we can use is one that we control.

Or one that God gives us. This is because this yardstick needs of necessity to remain constant, fair and immovable. When you approach self worth this way, you become sure of the person you are and the person you are becoming. Your process of predicting and planning for transformation becomes tangible and you begin to stay calm in the midst of storms. It is possible to remain calm through hardship, despair, accusation or failure. Likewise, good times and exciting achievements don't throw you off balance because your self-value is anchored on a secure and firm foundation.

I have had to question myself as often as I can in order to get here. It's the best way to realize your biases in measuring your true self value. Let me ask you some of my questions. Do you believe you are worthy? Do you believe you deserve the best in everything? The answers to these questions reveal a lot about your self-concept growth. If you hesitate to answer in the affirmative the fact is you don't believe you deserve or are worthy enough.

To illustrate my point let me ask: Do you believe that God loves you unconditionally or do you think you have to work for it? Do you believe you should be rich or there are just reasons in your mind for you to be at the income bracket you currently are in? Do you believe that you can be healed of any disease or according to you science has not yet proved that fact? Do you believe that you are the best or there is always somebody better? Since you were not born knowing fear and insufficiency, when did you learn you don't deserve the best and are not worthy enough? Who taught you those limiting self concepts? The hesitation in answering these questions may be momentary, but it reveals massive confidence disparities and self worth deficits.

On the converse, what is one area that you can answer affirmatively without hesitancy? Which question would you answer without twitching an eye? Look for that honest, sincere and truthful place from where you can answer this question without forcing the answer. That is where a healthy dose of self value residue is still residing. And that is a good place from where to begin the journey of self confidence recovery - from a pure deposit that is already your own. From this place of power now begin to build dominant thoughts of power, of love and of a sound mind in line with the spirit that God has given us.

Personal confidence is not merely about getting what you want; it also is about getting what you deserve. Many things accrue to you. Some will come because you want them. Others will come because you know they are yours. But a lot more will only come because you deserve them. Confidence is the journey to the discovery of what you deserve and more.

Many people know intellectually that they have good qualities. They have head knowledge but not experiential knowledge. They know they have achieved good grades or academic credentials. – but deep down they don't feel the same level of joy about themselves. That is why some high career achievers feel inadequate, sometimes worthless, and unlovable and struggle with feelings of shame and low self esteem. Intelligence does not always translate to confidence, and it shouldn't have to. If only intelligent people should feel confident, what about the rest?

With this kind of thought pattern or mentality, it is hard to feel worthy. It is impossible to feel like you deserve anything good. That is why we have to know how to calculate our worth

Motivation

Today, measure your value by your purpose. Build yourself towards your purpose. That is the only yardstick designed to calculate your value. Your purpose brings value to others. You are the most important resource to your purpose. And that should be where you direct all your value questions. If your purpose deems you valuable, then your worth is in the rightful place.

Today if your dominant thoughts are confident, relaxed, happy and certain of your success in purpose, then that is the blueprint for creating the unlimited life that you deserve! God not only wants you to get what you deserve, He wants you to get more than you deserve. Like a rich man buys caged birds to set them free, God has purchased you from low self worth so He can set you free. And if He let you fly, refuse to be a chicken!

You deserve so much more than you are currently giving yourself permission to see. You are worthy of every good thing that life has to offer. You deserve a permanent break from every enslavement mindset. Take that break right now! Look at purpose and keep your gaze there. That's where you worth is resident.

Inspiration

"Your value doesn't decrease based on someone's inability to see your worth." – Unknown

LESSON TWENTY

WHAT STOLE YOUR CONFIDENCE?

Confidence can be stolen. It can exist then be busted. It can be gained and it can be lost. It is possible to be strong then become broken. Such is the reality of the good things in life. We have to protect them and guard them daily. We have a responsibility to cover with prayer and every deliberate effort we can master, all things that we have been blessed with. And our confidence is one such asset that we must protect.

Children are not born scared, they learn fear. They don't know what it is to lack confidence until it is instilled into them through scares and harsh words by adults. They do not know what is bad until they are trained into the miserably stereotypical world of adults. Similarly, losing confidence happens during moments that leave is questioning our sanity and casting doubt on the fabric of our self confidence. There exists a plan in the unseen world to taunt, to crack and to weaken your confidence so that once the guard is lowered; an emotional attack becomes easily executable. And if we are not vigilant, it is very easy to discover we have been duped by life long after our confidence has been vandalised.

We have a duty every day to watch our interactions with situations, our reactions to occurrences and the effects we incur in relationships. Nothing leaves us the same: it will either add or subtract from us. Whenever we interact, one of the parts of us that is first to enter a situation or an interaction is our sense of confidence. By this reality alone, we know that our confidence can become a casualty if we are not trained on how to manage, direct and command situations. This battering of our confidence can have far reaching ramifications than we may immediately be aware of and far more than we bargained for. This is because a seared or scalded confidence continually becomes less sharp even in realizing its own compromise.

Do you recall any moment in your life when you lost your personal confidence? What happened at that point could be hindering not just your progress but also your ability to recognize potentially damaging situations to your confidence. A lost confidence may be affecting you more than you may imagine.

Sometimes we can lose confidence because of a traumatic experience. This happens more times than people may admit or even know. Emotional and psychological trauma is the result of extraordinarily stressful events that subtly shatter our sense of security, making us feel helpless, vulnerable and susceptible in a dangerous world. It can leave us struggling with upsetting emotions, shock, denial, or disbelief, confusion, difficulty concentrating, anger, irritability, mood swings, fear, guilt, shame, self-blame, hopeless memories, and anxiety that won't go away. It is worse in men because by their emotional structure, they may not want to express weakness, or show emotional need.

Men have been more shattered by emotional abuse, their own failure, ignorance and ego more than they can even describe. They have taken on so much emotional damage to the point that many of them in expensive suits, exotic cars and an endless company of beautiful girls are nothing but empty figurines of what they should have been by now. Women too have not been spared. Countless billions of women are hiding their broken confidence behind mascara, long lashes, Gucci hand bags and fake smiles. I couldn't imagine of a more tiring life than the fake existence of covering for lost confidence with perishable things.

Trauma can also leave us feeling numb, disconnected, and unable to trust other people. It can reduce life into a mechanical existence of inputs and outputs without our ability to actively participate in the process and the enjoying of creating the outcomes. Do you feel overwhelmed, isolated, frightened and helpless? You likely are suffering trauma. Whether your trauma was caused by a humiliating event or a deeply disappointing experience, it is hard to have confidence under these circumstances.

Confidence is about a total command and a resolute control over distracting anxious thoughts. An anxious mind makes us lose vital focus. And although anxiety can attack anyone, it doesn't have to control you. It is within our power, while armed with this kind of knowledge, to be able to direct life towards a direction that both favours us and builds our confidence at every interaction.

It is extremely important to be able to confess to ourselves that we have suffered a loss of confidence somewhere along the way. The question is, can you trace back to the place where your confidence fell? Much more important than falling, can you trace the place, the relationship, the job or the situation where you confidence began to stagger before it fell? We need to conduct an audit of our life to see what needs bandaging, what needs healing, what needs a miracle and what needs transformation. Confidence is critical! And we have to pay attention to it. But unless we identify where the rain began beating us, we cannot reclaim, restore or rebuild our confidence.

Motivation

Today, whatever the cause of your anxiety, trace it, identify it and address it resolutely and courageously. Seek professional counselling, or read a book to understand how to handle it. Seek help or confide in somebody that can help you be restored. Address what happened, observe how it changed you and begin working on your emotional and psychological wellness. Invest in your mental health diligently as much as your spiritual wholeness. Work back to the place you were before you lost your confidence then work from there to an even better emotional location. Work to have peace so you can control your world. You cannot undo what happened, but you can control its effects on you. Take back control! Confidence is refusing to lose yourself in the midst of overwhelming life's onslaughts. It is the awareness that despite pain, maltreatment, molestation, tragedy or even failure, we are always triumphant in all things no matter the outcome. We have a constant promise of victory even when some outcomes do not make sense!

Don't be controlled by the fear of failure, by what others said or didn't say about you, what worry is demanding you sink into or by other people's definition of happiness. Know what you want and go for it! Knowing what you want is a game changer! Know what you want; and go for what you want! Change your game from today!

Inspiration

Every time you are tempted to react in the same old way, ask if you want to be a prisoner of the past or a pioneer of the future.
~ Deepak Chopra

LESSON TWENTY ONE

YOU AND YOUR PROBLEM ARE TWO DIFFERENT THINGS

In life things do go wrong. If they haven't yet, they will. And sometimes, they can go very wrong. Tragedy, accidents and even catastrophes can hit leaving a trail of devastation and destruction like a tsunami in its wake. Such is life. There is no need to deny it or sugar-coat it. We all have a fair share of challenges and we all have bad days.

A great majority of human beings, with good intentions but perhaps in the deception of innocence take life's occurrences personally. They are unable to disassociate themselves with what happens to them. Instead of feeling pain, they experience the pain. Instead of seeing the anguish, they soak wet in it. Instead of standing at a distance to feel the heat of life's burns, they are unable to stand at a distance and watch the house burn. In the process they become too attached to temporal things and get scalded, scorched and burnt – sometimes beyond recognition.

Life is good. But life is also made up of trouble. God did not promise us a life devoid of challenges. Life is a game. And sometimes, life becomes a tournament. To expect trouble free existence is living in a dangerous illusion bubble. Furthermore, a life denuded of stress and stretching is like a meal without salt. Pain and discouragement are the spice of life. When life denies us something and after a tough battle of faith and grit the thing is released to us, we enter into a peak. We enjoy a highlight and a pinnacle of satisfaction. That moment becomes the joy of life, the break we long for, the reason for living and the reward for the battle.

Our passion for success should be proved by our insistent persistence and not the thirst for comforts and pleasures. Our intention for success is revealed in how we embrace challenges. We have to ask ourselves this question - What's my motive for success? Do I want impact, influence and power or am I seeking for attention?

Your worst moments do more for you than your best times. Your lowest moments build you more than your mountain experiences. Your celebrations count for a meagre role-play in comparison to your gruesome training, hardships and strenuous endurance. Your near-death moments add more life to you than all entertainments put together. Value the dark moments and be grateful that they came your way. They are the envelopes that delivered your tenacity and the post office that brought your package of power! Your pain is your friend; more than your fun will ever become. Your enemies do more for you than all your friends and family put together. Therefore, don't ask 'why me?' ask 'why not me?'

However, there is a danger when we are untrained on handling challenges. There is a mindset that rides the storms of life instead of drowning in them. And this kind of frame of mind knows how to separate us from what we are going through. It considers the two as different and separate. A confident mindset sees pain as temporary and itself as the permanent variable.

Confidence is about learning to separate life's outcomes from the process of those outcomes. For instance, confident people view failure as an event and not a person. They don't see achievement as a destination but as a stepping stone. This is how confidence is clothed in humility. Confidence helps us to not be attached to specific outcomes so that we remain able to build from glory to glory without losing enthusiasm. And whether we are being accosted by pain or glory, confidence knows how to strike the place of balance which in turn allows us the safety of not being drowned by any outcome.

While in uncertain times, the fear of the unknown can leave us navigating through life by simply going along with the current. Without deliberate confidence in what we want, it is inevitable to allow outside forces to determine our direction. Whenever we open ourselves up to the process of learning, suffering or sudden success is forced to bear great wisdom that can guide us into unbelievably golden revelations and enriching experiences. We can soar in the storm instead of inundated by it.

The confidence of success is such that we are required to wake up and be present in our own lives, to participate in our own making and to b**ecome conscious of why we do what we do. Discovering the reason – your reason for being here, is a game changer. If the 'why' is clear, the how will bow down and yield success. We have to stay awake and not allow anything to** tranquillize us. When this reality fully dawns on us, it makes us unstoppable!

Confidence in the process of success is also about opening ourselves and our mentality up to prosperity. It informs us to not be so uptight, rigidly clinging to the methods and the ways of life that are familiar. It is about starting to think of ourselves as a success, a**ccepting that personal progress is not linear and being at peace when riding the waves and the storms on our way to greatness. Confidence in the process of success is about** actively and repeatedly trying to escape comfort zones by persistent and deliberate practice!

Confidence pushes us to focus on the process and manage to enjoy it, to slice big goals into smaller targets each with time frames, tasks and mini rewards and to celebrate small victories and milestones as and when we achieve them. It is about staying upright in moments when life demands we crash and burn. Without this kind of mind, it is easy to be swallowed up by the intense moments of life. Confidence reminds us that our God is the Alpha and the Omega but He is also everything else between. He is a present help through all of life's processes. *"Success is liking yourself, liking what you do, and liking how you do it."* -- Maya Angelou

Motivation

Today, make peace with the route that life has taken you. You passed through hell's gate and hell's kitchen but you are here now. You were born in poverty and disadvantage but you cannot change that. You didn't finish your degree and your credentials or the lack of them; always scream in your face. You cannot travel back into time and change that either. But there is one thing you can change – your destiny! Stop fighting and resisting; embrace your life as it is. Stop the regrets and the wishful thinking. It is what it is. Stop rehearsing and studying your weaknesses and begin to study your strength. There is no amount of fire, pain, poverty, disadvantage or hardship that can abort your destiny. None!

If you will focus on your strength and greatness, you will become everything you desire and more. But you have to constantly remind yourself that you are not what happened to you. You and your failure are two different things.

Inspiration

Forget about what's happened; don't keep going over old history. Be alert, be present. I'm about to do something brand-new. It's bursting out! Don't you see it? There it is! I'm making a road through the desert, rivers in the badlands. Wild animals will say 'Thank you!' —the coyotes and the buzzards— Because I provided water in the desert, rivers through the sun-baked earth, Drinking water for the people I chose, the people I made especially for myself, a people custom-made to praise me.

LESSON TWENTY TWO

WHERE IN LIFE DO YOU RANK YOURSELF IN YOUR MIND?

We all have an unconscious self concept that dictates how and where we see ourselves in relation to others. Besides that, we also have an actively evaluating system in us that constantly seeks to gather information about people we meet for the first time, so we can determine where to classify them in our mind. We are both victims and also victimize others in this manner.

This may seem like a good emotional safety idea. It may make us feel a sense of security to a certain degree. But it is an erroneous way of measuring our place in the equation of confidence. First of all, the things that people use to determine honour are very materialistic. Secondly, the fleeting nature of such things means that our incalculable human value shouldn't even be measured with such temporal things. The problem is not in the measuring, but in what we use to measure, like we saw in chapter 19.

There is a basic minimum that we all should adopt when it comes to ranking ourselves in society. This ranking should be our own safety precaution – a measuring barometer – by which we know when we are undervaluing ourselves, lowering the bar of self concept or even when we are raising ourselves too far above what we are presently capable of fairly and genuinely managing. Furthermore, it is prudent to accept that there will always be younger, better, more beautiful, more talented and better earning people around us.

Confidence means believing in yourself even when other people look, sound and feel better than you. Sometimes, the grass looks greener on the other side, but greener grass could be planted on sewage. Confidence is self-endorsement in the correct proportions and balance – not selling yourself more or short of your true value. Healthy confidence sets expectations and fulfils those expectations within contentment and gratitude.

Confidence reminds you that you are not a success imposter: thereby training you to accept your increasing ability to succeed! Confidence reminds you that you are competent and therefore intermittent victory is not a sign of weakness but rather an indicator that you have found your niche. It reminds you to differentiate *yourself* from your mistakes: because you are not one and the same thing. It is confidence that allows you to embrace, enjoy and appreciate short term achievements, regardless of the amount of it in comparison to other people around you. Your success – big or small – is your success and must always be celebrated.

Confidence reminds you to **shift your daydreaming to the future, from the past, and get the job done today – right now – because you are well able! It reminds you of your** capability to organize and execute the courses of action required to manage prospective situations at any given time. It reminds you of your ability to succeed in all situations that you put your entire mind to! Confidence calls you back to action when giving up looks and feels more sizzling and tantalizing.

Ranking yourself accurately in your mind is critical. You have to be abundantly clear of the difference that you make and the difference that you bring. You have to be happy with yourself throughout the trajectory of your growth without putting undue pressure on your performance because of comparisons with other people. Knowing that you are the best changes everything. After all, there is no other you in all the earth. Nobody can be or do what you do in the entire universe. Such is your unique position and potential dominion, but it can only equate to value and power if you accept yourself as such. If you don't see yourself as valuable, nobody else is obligated to.

I rank first because I am first. My life has to begin with me because if it doesn't, who else is charged with that initiative? In my life, I rank top and not bottom; the head and not the tail. My mind is clear that I am my priority and my rank is non-negotiable. If this is not clearly established in my mind, even God has no authoritative position in me from where to influence the rest of my world.

My experiences obey my rank. My miracles are attracted by what I believe about myself. In fact, the size of the miracles that occur around me is commensurate to the size of my faith in who I am, in what I believe I deserve and the size of my mentality. My mind has become elastic to the elasticity of my rank. All this is because I have come to articulate this one phenomenal truth: without a clear definition of my self-value, life happens around me as though I was a pedestrian to it instead of the driver of it.

My proposition is this: define your rank in life. Assign value to your existence. Know yourself and teach your environment that lesson. Make everything and everyone around you adapt to your empowered self-concept. Welcome everything that builds that and disallow everything that weakens it. Your self-concept is a great treasure. It determines the mood, and the temperature of your entire life. Work on it from now!

Motivation

Today, pray that God reveals to you your purpose! In that purpose, locate yourself at the top of it in every way! That is your legal rightful place in this life. Envision what a great day will look like, ten years from today in your purpose! See yourself as the man of the day or the woman of the day in that grand celebration. Then pull that moment to today and begin treating yourself that way from today. You already are what you hope to be in ten years time; you just haven't acknowledged it yet.

Every time you catch yourself thinking of the past, of regrets and unmet expectations, shift your thoughts to that vision you created—then make plans to make that dream come true every day. Every time your vision shifts from your true self to the pressure and distress of present moments, refocus your eyes on whom you are and not on what is happening. Things that happen should not make you; you should make things happen!

Today, Recover quickly from setbacks and disappointments and view challenging problems and malignant challenges as tasks to be mastered! **Your self-beliefs become self-fulfilling prophecies. Prophesy power and success over yourself!**

Begin to develop a deeper more meaningful interest in the vision tasks in which you participate. Stop dwelling on problems and begin dwelling on solutions. Form a stronger sense of bond and commitment to all your interests, investments, goals, daily schedules and plans. Be present in your life. Don't drive your vision by remote control. You deserve the best. But more importantly, the best deserves you!

Inspiration

Blessed be GOD— he heard me praying. He proved he's on my side; I've thrown my lot in with him. Now I'm jumping for joy, and shouting and singing my thanks to him. GOD is all strength for his people, ample refuge for his chosen leader; Save your people and bless your heritage. Care for them; carry them like a good shepherd.

LESSON TWENTY THREE

WHAT ECO-SYSTEM HAVE YOU CREATED FOR YOUR SUCCESS?

I enjoy observing people and their behaviour. It reveals a lot about how humans think. Lifestyle patterns reveal the templates that govern mentalities and if you can observe people long enough, you will understand what drives their outcomes. I have observed closely two types of people in their advanced age; those who actively take care of their bodies in their younger years and those who don't. Over time, physical exercise begins to pay back in form of mental aptness, general health and physical appeal. As a direct and observable example, this is the same way in which investment in our emotional space rewards us. The bank in which we deposit emotional currencies eventually allows us to withdraw that same currency that we deposited.

The reality of life is this: we live in the environments that we create. We are animals in our own zoos. We always inevitably become victims or beneficiaries of the emotional houses we built. Positively or negatively charged environments have different effects on us, but at the end of the day, we hold the tools that cultivate the environments we live in. This is an inescapable eventuality; we ultimately experience what we have permitted. Let that sink.

Hope, joy, love, anger, faith, abuse, tension or doubt are all environments that can exist around us. They are realities that prevail if we let them. The good thing is that we get to choose what environments germinate, thrive or even exist around us in the first place. Life is encapsulated in the words of God – ***"I place before you Life and Death, Blessing and Curse. Choose life so that you and your children will live."***

God is not responsible for the way you end up; you are. We determine the temperatures of our associations, the warmth of our love, the pain of our regrets or the fertility of present moments in giving us a better future. We are not always victims of our environments; we also have a say in the formation of these emotional neighbourhoods. We knowingly or unknowingly participate in the creation of these events. Taking charge of destiny begins by acknowledging this fact.

Besides that, we also have our own internal layers upon layers of emotional turmoil. We have these internal battles and sometimes wars that inevitably shape how we view ourselves long before we even open our mouths to say anything. This combination of internal and external environments has a huge impact on the kind of person we continually become. These two factors need very careful monitoring to ensure we are creating our own cheer leader platforms and we are not silently becoming our own worst enemy. We have to be on own side in all things. The shaping of our environments, though subtle, eventually shows in the strength or weakness of our confidence.

Let us observe this thought a little further.

Every human being suffers from negativity bias. This is an inherent trait of leaning towards losses more than opportunities or the tendency to dwell more on mistakes instead of successes — on doubt more than on faith and on fear more than courage. This has a direct effect on our eventual emotional formation.

This is where confidence steps in. Confidence is about the courage to swiftly face and neutralize these soul suggestions, thoughts, emotions, notions, imaginations and anxieties that push us outside of our zone of peace, joy and thereby edging us out of our productivity. Without the ability to manage our environments, we slowly lose the power to lead ourselves into victories. And without a continuous progress towards victory, we regress into victimhood — in one way of the other.

Confidence does not do well in toxic environments; it thrives in positive emotions. The good thing is that positive emotions have an out-doing effect on anxiety thereby restoring confidence to its ideal environment within a short moment. That means that armed with this knowledge, we are at an advantage. When negative bias threatens our stability, we need to quickly bring into play our positive emotions of joy, excitement, calmness, peace and serenity. When doubts kick in, we have to quickly call forth faith! This promptly restores both our confidence and our focus on what is good and beneficial. And when we master this self control, we give confidence a chance to lead us in the places where success awaits us.

Confidence chooses what to think about. It decides what to imagine, what to choose and what to shun. We have a job to create positively charged environments around us. We have a duty to create healthy atmospheres with our words, actions, attitudes and behaviour. Even our faith in God functions at its optimum when we have conducive environments – environments of love, peace, and joy and possibility mentality.

The Garden of Eden was a meeting room between God and man. It was a controlled environment where thriving was automatic. In it was no shame, embarrassment or fear; confidence reigned! Today, God's Word comes to create that type of environment. It comes to build our confidence. It comes to encourage and empower. Whenever we find ourselves losing the grip of our confidence, something else is at work other than God. And we must resist it with all our might. Preserving our atmosphere of confidence is a duty we have to take up every day with vigilance and understanding.

Motivation

Today, create the environment that inspires you. You don't have to be subject to anyone's negativity; you can be the leader of your own space. Surround yourself with joy, love and peace. Listen to the melodies that calm your nerves. Have a good hearty laugh. Play the sounds that heal your troubled soul. Visit the places that keep you energised and rejuvenated. Avoid toxic people and situations. Forgive quickly and be at peace as much as you can. Give your confidence the food and the drink that it craves. Don't trade your confidence for anything!

Today choose your thoughts, decide what to dwell on and select who is worth your time and emotion. Pray over your mind and sustain its health with worship. You need to live in a healthy space. But a healthy space is forcefully and actively created!

Inspiration

Summing it all up, friends, I'd say you'll do best by filling your minds and meditating on things true, noble, reputable, authentic, compelling, gracious—the best, not the worst; the beautiful, not the ugly; things to praise, not things to curse. Put into practice what you learned from me, what you heard and saw and realized. Do that, and God, who makes everything work together, will work you into his most excellent harmonies.

LESSON TWENTY FOUR

HAVE SELF-COMPASSION

We all want to appear caring or concerned about other people. At least most of us who are not narcissistic and sadistic brutes do. We genuinely feel the affliction of others and our compassion is triggered by their pain. We may act or not act depending on circumstances but the truth is we have compassion.

My observation is that a lot of people show more compassion outwards than inwards. We are more likely to act to help other people in distress, especially people we love, but we rarely accord our own selves that same concern, care and attention that our emotions need. Now, don't confuse what I am saying with pampering the body with a massage, sauna or going out for a meal; I am talking about genuine emotional care and hospitality. Very few people know how to take good care of their soul. Consequently, a lot of people have had their confidence badly bruised because their mind, will and emotions have been run like a car without service.

One powerful way to build confidence is by practicing self-compassion. Self-compassion means to constantly have our own best interests at heart. By this I don't mean selfishness, but the balanced love for self. This way we learn to support ourselves in the same way that we would support a friend or a leader or a relative. Self-confidence helps us engage fully with life from a personal point of view. It also helps us realize that we will be alright regardless of the ups and downs we have in life. Self love is what makes this possible. But how many times do we even stop to think about this? When is the last time, for instance, did you counsel yourself in a crisis or healed your soul in a storm? Perhaps you think that is God's work. No it is not. It is your work.

A lot of people are imprisoned in a men-pleasing cycle – a cycle with the worst form of self-abuse. Men pleasers 'borrow to buy' things (emotional and material) that they don't need, just to impress people who don't like them in the first place. This massively erodes self confidence. It is not different from emotional abuse as we know it. Self compassion positions us at the healthy spot in the garden of life where we are nourished first, loved first and built first – before we can feed, love or build anybody else.

The reason why we have to begin from loving ourselves before we can love others is because we cannot know the measure of love that others need, until and unless we have experiential knowledge of the same. Compassion is not theoretical; it is practical. You cannot give what you do not have. And the gift of compassion needs to be experienced before it can be given. To be a doctor to others but a patient to yourself does not work. A true doctor needs to learn what it feels like to be sick and to be healed before he can attempt to heal the sick.

Recently when there was uproar in the entire world about Black Lives Matter, a pastor friend of mine who is white got really disturbed. I know his genuine love for people and i have watched him love God's people passionately. But this matter disturbed him at such a high level in his heart that because he had never been black in his life, he felt unqualified to address the matter even to some of us who are close to him. I remember vividly his post of social media asking his Black friends to teach him how to love them. It was extremely moving when he wrote me an apology for how black people had been treated.

My pastor friend did a tremendous act. He proved love and demonstrated it to his black friends and to the church he leads. But what remains with me forever is that from that day, I have never looked at him the same way. Whenever he speaks to me, I trust him more. In my observation, he sought to be 'sick' in order to heal. And when our afflictions became his afflictions, we were able to trust him as a healer. I believe that he has this wisdom: that to show compassion you must first feel what compassion heals.

To put ourselves in the shoes of others really does take much more than information; it takes experience. If we can feel the pain of others, the process we undertake to heal that pain in us, is the same as the process it takes to heal it in other people.

Self compassion is the foundation we need in order to qualify to help others. If we have no experience of self compassion, then what we give others is nothing more than pity at best and a bother at worst.

Our confidence depends a lot on our ability to show self compassion. When we take time to search out and heal broken places in our hearts, it boosts our confidence exponentially. We need time to correct our own erroneous mentalities, stinking thinking, disproportionate affections, racial biases, justified injustices, illicit intimacy, selfishness and emotional violence against others and against ourselves. This heals our guilt and when guilt is washed away, confidence stands out. We don't have to wait until somebody confronts our inordinate tendencies, self compassion helps us heal ourselves through self correction and self love at a friendly pace.

Motivation

Today, take yourself out on a coffee date for yourself and by yourself. Go on a drive, a nature walk or an ice cream treat. Consider what you need, what makes you happy and what needs attention in your personal life. Fix the conflicts and the turmoil that is boiling inside you. Give yourself attention before you donate it elsewhere. Without your ability to demonstrate self compassion, you probably don't qualify to give it to others.

Inspiration

... Love the Lord God with all your passion and prayer and intelligence and energy.' And here is the second: 'Love others as well as you love yourself.' There is no other commandment that ranks with these.

LESSON TWENTY FIVE

DON'T EXPECT PEOPLE TO KNOW YOU IF YOU DON'T KNOW YOURSELF

Allow me to emphatically say that self-concept clarity is the beginning of a lot your personal miracles. Without a clear picture of who you are and what you want, life cannot yield much to you. And it is not obligated to.

The journey of personal power cannot begin without a high self esteem and self esteem cannot be defined without **a clear sense of yourself and your ability to know who you are.**

Self-concept speaks of the set of beliefs you have about yourself. In this case, I am not talking about the "good" and the "bad" or the "pros" and the "cons" of being you, rather, the accurate assessment of your personal traits or attributes, the roles you play at work, in relationships or generally in your interactions, and the memories you have - your past experiences. These things point out a certain thing in you that you may not be consciously aware of.

For us to boldly say we have a clear sense of self concept, we have to be able to define with confidence – our self beliefs (our persuasions), be consistent in those beliefs (be steady in acting in line with our beliefs despite changing circumstances) and stay stable (not give in to the temptation to change to fit in another emotional container). We have to test ourselves over a period of time by staying immovable about our beliefs and maintain focus without fluctuating or wavering. For instance, you cannot believe in God this year, and then change in the next. Such fluctuation is not an indication of God's inability to prove Himself; it is about your lack of integrity in staying consistent in your own belief structure.

Besides proving your ability to be consistent, a clear self concept is undoubtedly associated with lower levels of depression and lower levels of anxiety. Besides reigning over their loneliness and stress this group of people also tends to enjoy more meaningful relationships.

I have a challenge with a lot of people in this area. Most people are more knowledgeable about their favourite celebrities, food, destinations, pop culture, sports **and other things more than they are with themselves. They have such a clear understanding of things that don't matter while**

neglecting *self-concept clarity.* This is a clear indication of a worrying human trait: the scope of people's ignorance is often invisible to them. Indeed, even jailed criminals think they are more kind, more trustworthy and more honest than the average member of the public

In attempting to help us better understand the importance is this idea, I m not talking about self-flattering beliefs of how 'better than others' we should feel, I am talking about taking time to honestly self reflect, invest and monitor the growth of the most important human being in the universe – you! Without this clarity, we are wasting time trying to be significant. Without this alignment to our core essence, we are building castles in the air – busy but with no outcomes or incomes to show for it. Without it we may smile outwardly but deep inside, we are broken and emotionally broke. Here are a few tips on clarifying your self-concept.

Are you able to separate your motions from your decisions?

How do you respond to life's frustrations?

What kind of person are you attracted to in a love relationship?

What behaviour in a partner have you fallen prey to most often?

How do you respond to a lot of money or little monetary income?

What are you talented in? What your most valuable talent or gift?

Do you have a taste for a good life or you are just okay with anything?

The clarity of self concept is directly related to our level of confidence. Confidence is about a constantly healthy self perception – both knowing it and sharpening it. But self perception is unlikely to improve without gratitude towards presently known advantages, unique traits and inherent capabilities – while fully cognizant of our weaknesses, evil tendencies and character. Gratitude massively improves self confidence because it recognizes and honours our tools and skills, presently available and usable, to create immediate change in any emotional area.

When we recognize and appreciate what we have, we give it permission to exist. We allow it to express its fullest value. We unlock its maximum content! And it begins to thrive! Confidence is having the tools to create instant conduciveness for our maximum productivity. When we don't recognize what we already have, we postpone the joy of confidence. And when we do not know what we don't have, we bank on non-existent resources to tackle real problems.

Motivation

Today, work on the clarity of your self-concept. Who are you when nobody is watching? And who are you to you? Take time to self-interrogate and build a firm picture of who you are and what you are capable of. Appreciate your emotional, mental, psychological and spiritual advantages and watch your confidence improve. Focus on your strengths, your advantages, your abilities and what uniquely gives you a head start over and above others. You are advantaged in something. Do you know it? In your advantage is your greatest reward. In your dominant gift is your prosperity! But clarify your self-concept. That is the first step towards thriving.

Inspiration

... by the grace (unmerited favor of God) given to me I warn everyone among you not to estimate *and* think of himself more highly than he ought [not to have an exaggerated opinion of his own importance], but to rate his ability with sober judgment, each according to the degree of faith apportioned by God to him.

LESSON TWENTY SIX

DO YOU RADIATE CONFIDENCE OR TIMIDITY?

People observe you every day. Aware or unaware, you are under constant surveillance and scrutiny. Unaware even to them, they are picking tiny pieces of information within seconds of meeting with you to evaluate if you are a threat, an ally or prey. They are evaluating you - interpreting your appearance, character, confidence, words, composure, attitude and temperament. Human beings are so advanced that they will subconsciously pick even the inaudible and unobservable magnetisms of thoughts and mindset emitted by your subconscious mind. That's how you meet somebody for the first time and they treat you in a certain way that people that know you treat you. They are looking at what you are exuding in order to calculate how they should treat you. In the world of confidence, prey attracts predator and confidence attracts respect.

Have you ever wondered why you always attract the same kind of men or women? Are you familiar with the frustrated utterance 'all men are the same'? No they are not. Good men and women are out there; they just don't feel attracted to you. The problem is not with them; you probably should consider that you are the common denominator in all of the similar relationships that didn't work out.

Whether we understand it or not, admit it or don't, there is an air – an atmosphere or an aura that hangs around each one of us. Everyone has a perfume – so to speak. We either flow within the air of unshakeable confidence or are spiralling within a whirlwind of uncertainty. But we are atmosphere carriers – bearing our own life's signature.

Our thoughts communicate. Without opening our mouths, our thoughts say things about us. Yes, they snitch on us. Without singing a song or uttering anything in any known language, our thoughts tell a story. This story is the story of our internal power or defeat, our fear or courage, our confidence or intimidation. Even in our silence, our thoughts speak statements; they make utterances and prophecies. Thoughts are energies: negative or positive which can be felt by those around us. As a man thinks so is he.

On the other hand, intimidation is real. We sometimes feel dwarfed in the presence of people we consider better than us. We feel so little that sometimes we unknowingly hand over our power to them, not because they are greater or better, but because of how we feel about ourselves in their presence. But just like our confidence should never come from intimidating others, nobody should feel empowered by your timidity in their presence. The fact of the matter is, if we do not stop ourselves from feeling intimidated by people's imaginary powers, and if we do not stop considering others as intimidating, we will always give them our power.

The dictionary defines 'to intimidate' as 'to threaten someone in order to suppress his will to act out of his own discretion by making him feel threatened, or to coerce him to do something which he does not wish to do.' But when you look closely at this definition, something is incomplete in that definition.

Normally we feel more intimidated than we intimidate people. Actually, we normally attempt to intimidate people who intimidate us. My point is that intimidation is more of our own feeling than it is another person's. We feel inferior around certain individuals. We feel unable to do what we want and unable to express ourselves freely – fearing judgement or mistreatment. Yet, all these feelings are imaginary fears created by a low self confidence within us. A lack of self-love and the self awareness of who we truly are is the root cause behind a person's insecurities. People's actions, inactions or behaviour ought to have no bearing whatsoever with how you think and feel. What you feel and think should only be determined by you and not by others.

The main reason why we feel worthless or valueless is because we compare ourselves with people that we deem superior to us in one way or another. It is this comparison that makes them look intimidating and even superior to us. In psychological terms, feeling intimidated is really due to a lack of control over our own ability to think constructively, compare objectively, decide independently, understand without bias, imagine without prejudice and contemplate life from a position of personal dominion. The only person you should compare yourself to is the person you were yesterday; not those around you today.

On the other hand, we have to learn to guard our own confidence from being contaminated by the insecurities of others. The nature of confidence is that it is contagious; but so is the lack of it. It is impossible to stay around uninspired people and be inspired. To be in a room with emotionally undisciplined people can spell doom for your day, your next business, your relationship or your spiritual growth. This means that the progress you want to achieve every day requires a closely monitored atmosphere of peace! Volatile, bile-filled and negatively charged people should not be welcome in that space.

Now, I am not saying that we will not encounter emotionally stressed people; no! But when we encounter them, we need to remember that we are not obligated to become part of their turmoil. We can spectate but we don't have to participate. We can help but we don't have to partake of their indiscretions. We can sympathise and empathise but we don't owe them pity or an explanation why we won't stay around them.

Without a deliberate budgeting of our thought and emotional expenditure, we risk running down our own emotional bank account. With a depleted or negative emotional account, our own confidence begins to be eroded. And with each erosion comes loss, retrogression and self doubt. That is not a road you want to travel: its destiny is always downwards. Guard your confidence the way you would a valued investment. Stay away from emotionally irresponsible people. And if practically needed to, make every effort to. It may appear snobbish, but again, you owe nobody an explanation.

Besides this, we need to appreciate the nature of confidence in order for us to build our own. Confidence closely resembles faith: it's based on believing something you don't know with certainty yet you should do it before it can begin to work in you. Confidence does not mean that we are better than others or we have everything figured out, or that we even know ourselves completely; it means that we act boldly in spite of what we have or don't have. Confidence means that we continually and consistently develop our sense of self to the place where insecurities, unhealthy self-consciousness, emotional dependence on others, inability to stand up for ourselves, our crippling fears, our inferiority complexes and our people-pleasing attitudes wither and die off. Without these, we may never acquire an awareness of who we truly are, regardless of how we compare or measure up to others

Confidence is not a mere internal atmosphere balance, it also is about what we predominantly exude. For instance: - assertive posture, power poses, and appropriate eye contact decide a lot of the confidence game. A straight back, a confident walk, raised head, looking up instead of down, firm handshake, locking and maintaining eye contact, and gesturing with an open hand, palm facing up – all these have miraculous effects on others. These communicate acceptance, openness, frankness, sincerity, candidness, cooperation and trustworthiness, and serve as an indication that we don't feel anxious, nervous, or afraid. People who are not able to maintain eye contact or are the first to break eye contact indicate that they're hiding something, feeling uncomfortable, or projecting a lower-status than or submissiveness to the person they're speaking with. Mike Tyson one of the greatest boxers of all time says he would accurately predict almost all of his matches when he first looked his opponent straight in the eye. If his opponent blinked first, Tyson knew the game was already decided in his own favour.

Motivation

Today, exude confidence! Clothe your entire self with confidence. Practice smiling – it not only makes you more attractive and trustworthy, it also improves your health, your stress level, and your feelings about yourself. **Give a firm handshake and** Stop fidgeting. Inspire respect by practicing the confidence body language. Today, remember that the best confidence designer is walking in truth, integrity, being honest and sincere – staying away from guilt and character taint of every kind, as much as you can

Your emotional wellbeing is a resource; not a luxury. Your confidence is a need not a want. Your faith is a-must-have-asset and not a disposable feeling. Your success is more important than allegiance to emotionally incapacitated friends or relatives. Your significance is much more valuable than any relationship that doesn't add to you power, love and a sound mind. God has not given us a spirit of fear; but of love, of power and of a sound mind! Guard what He has given you.

Today remind yourself that you are a lion: so stop asking the opinion of sheep. Develop your confidence patiently, consistently and unapologetically. It will work, if you will put in the work. Your confidence is your power. Retain it. Never hand it over.

Inspiration

Do not, therefore, fling away your fearless confidence, for it carries a great *and* glorious compensation of reward. For you have need of steadfast patience *and* endurance, so that you may perform *and* fully accomplish the will of God, and thus receive *and* carry away, and enjoy to the full what is promised.

LESSON TWENTY SEVEN

WHAT LEVEL OF MENTAL RESILIENCE DO YOU POSSESS?

Our mind plays a very key role in the shaping of our every day experiences. It stands out as the organ of perception, the feeler that gathers information from our surroundings and the tentacle that stretches to smell the future, to analyse before we make a move. It also compares our intentions with past experiences to chart the best course of action. That means, in the most part, we cannot go where our mind hasn't been and we cannot travel to the places that our mind has not approved. We are locked within this consistent insistence on what we have thought and imagined within the constraints of the known reality. We tend to shy away from experiences that our mind is not familiar with and similarly, we find ourselves more confident to do what the mind deems possible, harmless or safe.

This is the primary process through which the mind leads. But though primary, the mind doesn't have to stay in this state otherwise our self-leadership will begin to degrade and our achievements would be relegated to our comfort zones alone. If we assume things will somehow change without paying attention to improving this fundamental determinant of life's attractions, we take too great a risk. Without addressing this core process, a strain begins to develop on our ability to make our success possible.

Mental resilience is the ability to stilt the mind, to enhance its performance, to support its functions and build its processing power so that it doesn't crumble under the pressure of life. *Mental Strength* is the capacity to deal effectively with stressors, pressures and challenges and perform to the best of ability, irrespective of the circumstances in which we find ourselves (Clough, 2002). It is also the ability to strengthen our 'risk-taking' taste buds so that life does not lock us up at the place where comfort is assured.

In faith-filled words, mental resilience is learning to be quite content whatever your circumstances. It is being just as happy with little as with much, with much as with little. It is finding the recipe for being happy whether full or hungry, hands full or hands empty. Whatever you have, wherever you are, you can make it through anything through knowing and functioning in the power of who you are.

Building mental strength is central to living our best life. Without it, spheres of our existence suffer in one way or another. Without it, potential can never be fully exploited and we risk mechanically living life. Although we are not all the same we all have areas we quickly bounce back from setbacks and other areas in which we struggle to get our groove back. Some people around us could also be better than us in recovering from challenges or in managing thoughts and negative situations. All these factors ought to be leveraged while we build our confidence.

Mental strength involves developing daily habits that build mental muscle. It also involves giving up bad habits that hold you back. - Morin

It is not possible to enjoy confidence without adequate mental resilience. This is because we don't only need to feel confidence when things are all pleasant and calm, but also when life takes a dip towards pain, shock and distress. Mental resilience is our own process of adapting healthily in the face of adversity, trauma, tragedy, threats or to be precise, handling well any significant sources of stress. It is our capacity to deal effectively with tension, anxiety, strain, pressures and challenges and yet perform to the best of our ability, irrespective of the circumstances in which we find ourselves.

"*Resilience,*" is actually a term borrowed from engineering that refers to the ability of a substance or object to spring back into shape after high tension or stress. Mental resilience helps us keep focus and determination. It helps us remain unwavering in the face of insurmountable challenges through the building blocks of Faith thinking, anxiety management, vision and visualization, imagination, prayer, goal-target-and-deadline setting and through attention and focus control.

There is no better builder or tester of resilience than an unanticipated change of the norm, and particularly towards a worse direction. Resilience is often tried when circumstances change unpredictably and for the worse — the death of close people, the loss of a job or investment, or the end of an important relationship. Such challenges drown a lot of people but to the resilient mind these present the perfect opportunities to rise above and bounce back stronger. The resilient mind has a mantra – every setback is a set up for a comeback!

It is mental resilience that helps us bounce back from personal failures and setbacks. And this is besides aiding us to take risks, try new things, and cope with difficult, even impossible situations. God has allowed us this incredible trait but we have the responsibility to hone it and train it through practice, discipline and hard work. The brain is a muscle that needs to go to the gym every day. Confidence is the proof of this kind of gym.

When we train our mental resilience, we need to focus on such areas as -

Self-control: the extent to which we feel we are in control of our life, including our emotions and sense of purpose.

Commitment: This addresses our personal focus and reliability - setting goals and achieving them, without getting distracted

Challenge Mentality: This is the extent to which we are self driven, adaptable and the ability to view change as an opportunity instead of threat.

Facing fears head-on: this is comfort in discomfort or the ability to feel comfortable in our own skin at any particular time

At the end of this self-analysis it's important to do an audit of your own mental resilience. Where do you stand in your ability to forge past hard times? How do you view problems? How do you react to rough patches? How do you respond to a bad day when things don't seem to work in your favour? How do you align yourself to the goals that you set until you see them come to fulfilment? Your mental resilience is one of the core gates that stand between your vision and the realization of that vision. Without tough, resistant and elastic mindsets, we are doomed into emotional slavery and mental prisons. Don't be a prisoner of something that you can change beginning this moment.

Motivation

Today, have confidence! Position yourself at the driver's seat of your thoughts, feelings, actions, reactions, responses, behaviour and as the head of your social neighbourhood. You are not a victim! There is nothing wrong with you! you just need to adjust your mind based on this information. Remember you are well able to create something great for your life. Don't work within the limitations of seeking to be loved and to find acceptance, step out of that comfort zone and do what needs to be done! Don't buckle under trouble or crumble under pressure. We are never alone: we have a Greater One in us! He is working to empower us past hurdle, beyond challenge and to total victory! Work with God today! Comply with His finger that is already at work with your hand!

You are victorious and triumphant in all things. Have the presence of mind to run your world! It will run if you will run it! If it has to be, it's up to you!

Inspiration

Don't fret or worry. Instead of worrying, pray. Let petitions and praises shape your worries into prayers, letting God know your concerns. Before you know it, a sense of God's wholeness, everything coming together for good, will come and settle you down. It's wonderful what happens when Christ displaces worry at the centre of your life.

LESSON TWENTY EIGHT

THE PROCESS OF BECOMING CONFIDENT

Outcomes are good. Without results we have no way to gauge or measure our progress. But this mentality is not entirely true. And this is my point.

When we become fixated on the outcomes, we forget the joy of the process and the purpose of the progression. Now, don't mistake me to mean that our focus should be on the process alone. My view is that the results and the means to the results are equally pivotal to our agenda. Confidence is about doing it well; not just about getting good results.

Results are subject to the process. The value of the process determines the worth of the results. And without this kind of mindset, we risk attaining great things but not becoming great men in the process. Without applying reverse engineering to this notion, we risk attaining success but not obtaining significance. Results are good. But the process is better. If we can master the process, we can get the results at will – any time, every time. Confident people know this secret. No wonder in their failures, they still smile as though they won; but if you think about it, they did indeed.

Confident people focus on the action instead of the outcome. They are independent of the result and not dependent on it. They are not defined by outcomes or incomes but by the quality of effort that they have to invest. This is the attitude that helps them keep breaking personal records until their record becomes better than everybody else's. Winning is not about one game, it's about the team. It's about the tournament. It's about the league. It's about a bigger picture than the mere pomp of a final whistle and a trophy in the cabinet. It's about the process we go through to become the worthy possessors of success. Success is merely the subject matter; it is a means to an end. The process is the object matter – the objective! What we become is much more important than the token of appreciation we receive at the end.

The grand glory is an accumulation of daily dwarf triumphs. This means that public honour comes from thousands of private efforts and those who are perfect only emerge from a journey of daily perfecting. What is "God-given" will require *thousands* of "man-hours" of hard work and practice spent perfecting and mastering it. Mastery has a price, and most people aren't willing to pay it. Success may be freely given but it is not cheap. And without this wisdom of confidence, we may neglect the process while rushing to collect profits and forget that the process is more profitable than the outcomes.

Our confidence is built while we practice, endure, focus, meditate, imagine, think, strategize, research, prepare and rehearse for our victories long before the day of victory. The practice process – the daily simulation and enactment of our greatness - is boring because there are no cheering squads involved. It is just us and the gym. But there is no other way to succeed. If we can get through the boredom of consistency, we can achieve truly enormous goals. Repetition can be uninteresting and monotonous. It can be dull and mind-numbing. Yes, I know it can get tedious, uninspiring and wearisome. And the inability of most people to handle this non-excitement period is what excuses them from eventual success.

Miracles do indeed happen when we focus on the process. Something divine begin to awaken in us when we view and turn our daily work into a consistently compelling and enjoyable performance! It is as if God notices our seriousness in the process He is taking us through. True champions focus on the process. They know that legends are not made in the ring—they're made in the gym; everyday for months and years before. They therefore train themselves to enjoy training. Likewise, if we spend more time practicing than competing, we ought to train ourselves to enjoy the place where we spend most of our time – in the practice and in the process. Don't wait for the finals to enjoy victory; enjoy today's practice session. In today's practice session, an instalment of victory has already arrived. You are a champion already. Though in the making; you still are a champion nevertheless.

The 'practice gym' trains your muscle, but it also trains your mindset. It begins to download and install the possibility frame of mind. As you engage more and more in the process, your mind becomes expanded from a spectator into a participant, and from a participant into a partaker. Before any competition, the frame of mind that we build during practice is really what overwhelms other competitors and subdues them on the day of competition to give us the crown. Skills play a part, but not the entire part. If we are skilled but not confident, our skill means nothing.

Mental resilience is more important than muscle resilience. Mental creation always precedes physical accomplishment. If, deep down, we don't really have the compelling belief that we are more than conquerors, we are practically guaranteed to fail. Worse still, skilled people are employed by confident people.

If we have 'won' in our mind already, success submits to that on the day of the match. Internal belief precedes external achievement. And it is this growing internal belief system that we call confidence.

God's wisdom teaches us a very significant lesson. Think about these words from the Bible. *"Consider it a sheer gift, friends, when tests and challenges come at you from all sides. You know that under pressure, your faith-life is forced into the open and shows its true colors. So don't try to get out of anything prematurely. Let it do its work so you become mature and well-developed, not deficient in any way."* Becoming sounds more important than being – process is more important than victory, even according to God.

When we focus on the process, we recognize that the

progression of success is really not about doing but becoming. An important life's lesson is this - we attract after our kind. We beget the things that look like us. That means if we are not developing, we have stopped becoming continuously deserving of better outcomes. Whenever we pay the full price for anything, we attach full emotional and psychological value to that thing. And whatever comes easy is naturally taken for granted.

The confidence to compete is incomplete if daily doses of it have not been taken according to prescription. Instant results don't build confidence. This is because when the result is instant, our participation is minimal, and if our contribution is little, we have no pride in the outcome. We don't own the outcome; something or someone else does. It doesn't take talent to succeed. If it did, then everybody would be successful. It takes confidence: the kind of confidence that is gained on the path of mastery.

The game of life has spectators and participants, it has champions and legends. Champions win trophies, legends win respect. Legends are not so because they are better than champions, but because they are compliant with every preparation necessary and are committed to the entire process on the journey to becoming the-greatest-of-all-time. They don't cut corners and try to make life more rounded, because they know shortcuts will cut them short. Participants are for games, champions are for leagues but legends are for life! What are you?

Process creates abundance mindset

Idris Elba, the London born actor of African descent, was recently named in the Time 100 list of the Most Influential People in the World. According to Wikipedia, as of May 2019, his films had grossed over $9.8 billion at the global box office, including over $3.6 billion in North America, where he is one of the top 20 highest-grossing actors. I am immensely impressed by this man of colour, not just because he is proof that colour means nothing in the game of greatness, but because of his consistently outstanding performance. I am intensely excited to see a towering role model whose ability to remain conspicuously relevant, in an extraordinarily competitive niche, demonstrating that any success is possible to anyone, colourism not withstanding. With such a record of screen appearances and television influence, Idris has a thing of two to tell us about abundance.

He describes the scarcity mentality in these terms - "The problem with a lot of people is that, if they get rejected by a job they want or a person they like, their self confidence becomes shattered in an instant because they don't have an abundance mindset. You see, when you have an abundance mindset and you get rejected, it's okay. Because you tell yourself tomorrow I will find 10 other jobs, or I will meet 10 other new people. You always have possibilities."

Abundance mindset is one of the rarest mentalities. It believes that there is more than enough of anything and there is adequate resource to go round for everyone. This mindset rejects notions of scarcity, jealousy and capitalism and lives in the possibility of even creating what is needed from what is invisible. Simply put, it is driven by vision and not by what is available. The exact opposite of this, the scarcity mindset, is what seems to flood our world today.

The ability to see abundance is a game changer. Our journey of confidence significantly depends on it. Options create a broad view point, they mitigate insecurity created by poverty, and by this we become psychologically freed from the burden of low self worth. Personal insecurity is terrible! I have suffered gross poverty and the devastating trauma of the low self value it births. I know what it means to feel invisible in the presence of people. I know what it feels to consider yourself irrelevant and inconsequential, long before anyone treats you as such. Poverty is of the devil!

Seeing abundance creates in us possibility thinking. It begins to draw a roadmap for us – out of defeat and squalor. When you know what is possible, you stop settling for what is available.

However, abundance is not merely the ability to see beyond the immediate scarcity and into the possible plenitude, we need to define current need accurately and in order to meet it sufficiently and effectively. What is that need that steals your confidence? And what is your strategy to defeat it permanently? We have to demonstrate that we are able to defeat evil with good – with precision. We have to overwhelm the enemies of our progress with a new-found quality of thinking that supersedes all their intended inventions to enslave us, even in the future. Confidence has to travel into the future and secure our dominion. Dominion is power over power, and if our confidence cannot overpower future threats, we are still not free. We need a plan to defeat what steals our confidence and defeat it so good that it never rises to ever breathe again!

If I were to ask you what your immediate need is on your journey to confidence, would you answer me in one word? Most people actually don't know what they need to do in order to improve their lives. They haven't studied their problem, and therefore cannot solve the low self value. They cannot tangibly describe what they want.

They are poor but have no plan or strategy to get out of poverty. They lament that the rich are thriving but criticize prosperity in the same breath. In my humble submission, I believe that part of the reason why people do not know how to meet their needs is because they do not know how to define what they need.

The ability to imagine your deficiency should have no limit. You ought to not only imagine your need but that of communities, families and nations around you. When you see need through the eyes of vision, you should have the access to the full image of what is missing. This way, you gain access into inside information about the supply that can be availed and the resources that can be dispatched to solve the entire problem and not just a little part of it. Your ability to see the entire need redefines your quest for a solution and energizes your passion to pursue the entire answer. And when you become this kind of irredeemably confident person, Heaven conspires to make your dreams come true!

Defining your deficiency

Let's think about this.

Imagine you are thirsty and you only have half a glass of water available right now. Most people calculate what they need by what is missing instead of seeing the fullness of what they require. Firstly what is in the glass is not the problem, what is missing is the problem. But secondly, abundant mindset leaders don't calculate need based on what they can see as insufficient, they count it on the thirst they need satisfied; not just for this moment but for the rest of their life. To meet the immediate need only reduces us to instant gratification problem-solving. A need is not what is lacking from the glass so the glass can be full: it is what is missing so we can quench the thirst for good. Furthermore, we shouldn't consider a need to have been adequately solved until we build a solution that solves that same problem for at least three generations. In the wise words of King Solomon, *"A good person leaves an inheritance for their children's children"*

What we have is merely a point of contact, an indicator of what we should have and what we could have. But our ability to calculate and define our need, based on the deficiency of what we have is what informs how much of it we should attract. I normally ask myself this question: 'John, how can God meet a need you don't know you have? How do you have a need that you cannot define?' an abundance mindset has taught me that my ability to define my need accurately is what attracts the need-meeting power of God. When you define your need, and spell it to Him, your need no longer stands against you, it stands against His riches in glory. He is able to supply what you define, to the tune of exceedingly, abundantly, above all that you can ask, think or imagine!

Part of our visionary capability is the skill to define need accurately. Vision is the ability to see the deficiency of what we have to the level conversant to the fullness, the wholeness and the completeness that God sees concerning that thing. It is moving from seeing it from what it is to what it could be. It is our ability to correctly decipher the amount of shortfall that is currently standing between where we are and where we ought to be. It is being able to see what is required to make us entire, complete, whole, with nothing missing and nothing broken. If we can define our need; our deficiency or what I call, 'the missing part', we begin to become need driven to the point that our solutions demand a whole new level of thinking. Meeting needs from an abundance mindset is what begets significance. And the more we can sharpen our ability to define the missing part, the better our chances of becoming significant solution givers. The more we accurately define need, the more our confidence to solve that need becomes.

Need is not for punishment, it is for the revealing of purpose, the unveiling of intention and the exposure of the plan of God that warrants the bringing of the resources of Heaven to earth. Need is a setup – an opportunity for us to grow our confidence levels. Without need on earth, Heaven is silent, Heaven is inconsequential and the resources of God have no work to do. But if we can be confident in bringing permanent solutions to every need around us, our reward becomes the very confidence we gain in the process. *Do not, therefore, fling away your fearless confidence, for it carries a great and glorious compensation of reward. For you have need of steadfast patience and endurance, so that you may perform and fully accomplish the will of God, and thus receive and carry away and enjoy to the full what is promised.*

This is the sum total of abundance mindset: What is in your hand at any given time is a seed; and not bread. It's the capital and not the profit. It's the beginning and not the end. It is merely the indicator before the turn. What you have is only a tip of the iceberg. But if you don't know that, you will only exist at the tip of life and never at the depth of the iceberg. Confidence thrives in an abundance mindset. It reminds us that we shouldn't view anything as permanent. Problems are temporary, and they have been given an assignment by God not to damage us, but to build our confidence!

Motivation

Today, earn your success. Incur the scars. Pay the price. Walk the entire nine yards. Bite the bullet. Employ competitiveness but deploy hard work. Work for it by giving it your best in what is required today and every day. Daily confidence is built on the premise of God giving us 'this day our daily bread'. Navigate past setback, failure, success and demands without losing enthusiasm. See perfection as joint efforts and eventual greatness as daily investments. Do today the best that you can and enjoy it. Enjoy the struggle. Measure the result, but focus on the process. Today remember that when we ask God for a staircase, He gives it to us in steps; one step at a time. Enjoy today's step! It's working for your good. And if you give it all it demands, it shall give you all it contains.

Inspiration

Define and enjoy the process. Don't forget all you have been taught and all that you have learnt; take to heart God's instructions of wisdom. They'll help you live a long, long time, a long life lived full and well.

Don't lose your grip on Love and Loyalty. Tie them around your neck; carve their initials on your heart. Earn a reputation for living well in God's eyes and the eyes of the people. Trust GOD from the bottom of your heart; don't try to figure out everything on your own. Listen for GOD's voice in everything you do, everywhere you go; he's the one who will keep you on track. Don't assume that you know it all. Run to GOD! Run from evil! Your body will glow with health; your very bones will vibrate with life!

Honour GOD with everything you own; give him the first and the best. Your barns will burst. Your wine vats will brim over. But don't, dear friend, resent GOD's discipline; don't sulk under his loving correction. It's the child he loves that GOD corrects; a father's delight is behind all this.

This is the process that births permanent confidence!

LESSON TWENTY NINE

CONFIDENCE IS ABOUT IDENTIFYING AND BUILDING OUR ADVANTAGE.

Confidence is the art of subtle confrontation; the ability to apply the psychology of negotiation without necessarily having to say anything but ending up with the controlling share. Confidence is the mastery of leveraging mind and behaviour to gain dominance in a setting or interaction with others. The mastery of this can be achieved by anyone. But not everyone attempts it. This is because most people prefer to live in the shadows of insignificance. They don't want to disturb the peace or ruffle any feathers. And so they go about their meagre lives affecting nothing, irritating nobody, upsetting no status quo, unsettling no generational curses and by being strictly compliant to peer pressure. What a wasted life!

The seed of greatness...

Every person carries an invaluable seed of greatness. We may call it potential, latent ability or dormant passion. We all have a capital of sorts – an investment that God placed in us as His gift to us on the day He sent us into the world. Potential is incalculable. It is unquantifiable. However, this world's system of thought calculates the value of men by their ability to amass wealth, build power and dominate others. But before we can even begin to calculate the value of a man's possessions, power and dominance, we may need to first calculate the value of the person that he is. And what better reference to consider than the words of the Maker of the man.

In God's own words – *"What good would it do to get everything you want and lose you, the real you? What could you ever trade your soul for? For what shall it profit a man, if he shall gain the whole world, and lose his own soul?"* What he is demonstrating to us here is that the value of one man is beyond what can possibly be payable. If the whole world could be sold, the proceeds could not be sufficient to purchase the soul of one man. God's valuation chart is truly out of our budget. We grossly err when we devalue people based on their poverty, struggles, inadequacies, pay grades or appearances.

Everyone is and has a gift to this world. Yes, even you! That means that in you is the potential to become something of a wonder. We all are walking marvels! We are peculiar miracles decked with pure amazement! We are a blank canvas on which strong, grand, awesome and monumental pictures can be drawn. The only reason your life is not yet beautiful is because you have not yet began drawing on your canvas. We are laden with explosive power that's silent and calm. We possess latent, dormant, inherent, unrealized and undeveloped power that is not even known to us yet. In its full exploitation, the potential of one man can radically change the course of the entire world.

We are designed to have or to show the capacity to develop into something in the future - a likely, prospective or probable future. By our desire to discover ourselves, we give permission to our future selves to begin manifesting. This is because the seed of greatness as long as it is seed, remains as potential. But when it is tapped, it unlocks the divine part in us.

In the world of science, some seeds lie dormant as a survival technique: they wait until weather conditions are optimal to make their big debut. It is a known fact that many wild plants have seeds that can remain dormant for many years before birthing a plant. Seeds can have an indefinite life and potential may not have an expiry date as long as we are alive.

On the other hand, the life of a seed can drastically and radically shift upon the change of the conditions or the environment in which they are placed. When a conduciveness for germination comes into play, this seed-full-ness, upon detection of the right atmosphere, converts the seed from potential into possibility! In the year 2005 a 2000-year-old date palm seed found in Israel actually sprouted when it was planted! Think about that!

A seed in the right conditions is no longer latent and dormant capability but it now has gained the right to become countable in terms of feasibility, practicability, chances, odds, attainability or achievability. It can now become a measurable, expected and deductible matter. It moves from an open-ended promise to a goal with a dead line. This is exactly what happens to you when you move your potential into the environment that is mandated by God to cause your germination.

This phenomena is what governs the life of every person. We carry latent and dormant capability and we do not begin to live life until we are able to convert 'a seed into a plant' and potential into possibility. The seed of greatness - talents, gifts and abilities - are only potential. But when it begins to be sowed, it graduates from potential to possibility. As soon as the seed changes location, from a store to a garden, the dynamics change so radically that what the seed couldn't become, it suddenly can become - because it's now located in the place of its manifestation.

Every potential is a foundation for self confidence

Every potential must be converted into prospect. This is what gives us hope and builds our confidence. This is the process through which we really grow. Without continual discovery of things that can dramatically change our experiences, our fire for life dwindles away. We have to constantly find unconverted potential sitting dormant in us and convert it every day. As we discover new places and powers within us, our confidence levels begin to shift too.

Unlocking the world of possibility is why we live. We exist to discover answers for questions and solutions for problems for other and for ourselves. We live to benefit and to profit the world. We are producers and not mere consumers! We exist to unlock the future with its power and pleasures! Our potential is a prophecy of the future and it is what unlocks our vision into a brighter future! When the future becomes unknown, people travel backwards into the known past where there is no vision, and where there is no vision people perish. Our work is to unlock potential, build possibilities until all things are possible. When we surround ourselves with beautiful and compelling options, we create advantage for ourselves. This in turn becomes our secret for accelerated advancement and the fertilizer for our self confidence.

Confidence is about locating and building our advantage. It is about identifying and paying attention to what is in our possession already that puts us at the lead. It is about carefully studying our strengths, our beneficial positions and the things that give us a head start ahead of other people. This awareness is literally the beginning of miracles. What we have, can at any time be leveraged for what we need.

Increased profits and advancement is about leverage. Without leverage, our overall outcome; the probability of grand gains or enormous rewards, is limited to our cumulative energy and input at best, or pure chance and luck at worst. Our effort is never enough – it can only get us so far. Hard work is good but it's not everything. But with the power of leverage, we can significantly gain that much-needed "edge" to command results that others only dream of. Confidence begins when we know what we have that others don't, and knowing how to use what we have to get what we need.

Leverage is one way to prove that we are deliberate about our pursuit of greatness. It gives us the advantage of a better springboard than what mere wishful thinking can ever do. However, the springboard on its own will not launch us into higher heights. We have to jump on the board to amplify our spring. In true essence the springboard uses what we have then makes it greater. If we don't jump on the board, he will remain stationary, common and average like everybody else. But the more we jump on the board – the more we leverage what we have - the higher the board will take us. An advantage is something that puts us in a better position than other people who don't have it. We have advantages. Let us search them out, discover them, utilize them and build our confidence in the process.

How are you using your unique strengths?

It beats the purpose of life for us to wallow and indulge in potential. It's unbecoming to pride ourselves in dormant power. It is a loss to settle at the mere thrill of threatening or inducing a false feeling of what can happen should we choose to unleash our potential. This is where many people live. Unfortunately, this is the village of cowards. Real men and women step out of the conform zones of mere threats into actions. They grow up from toys and staged episodes of success into making things happen! They are grateful for potential but their dream is to see the world of faith where all things are possible!

We must deploy faith! Fearless faith! And starve fear to death! The opposite of faith is not doubt; it is fear. Both faith and fear have power to create what each stands for. What we believe happens. And what we fear comes upon us. It is the opposite of trust that is doubt. And we cannot trust and doubt somebody at the same time. Faith works with trust while doubts work with fear. Whenever we begin to confront our insecurities by daring to exercise our faith, the personal confidence we crave begins to also stand up and speak.

Most people imagine greatness as a simple game of chance. They have no idea that greatness is carefully calculated success. We plan success thorough an accurate assessment of our capabilities. With the right tools at our disposal we can make massive differences for ourselves and others. People that use the proper leverage tools get far more in return than their inputs.

WHAT'S IN YOUR HANDS?

William Clement Stone was a businessman and philanthropist who overcame all odds to become one of the most celebrated American entrepreneurs of his time. According to Wikipedia, Clement's father died in 1905 leaving his family in debt. In 1908 he hawked newspapers on the South Side of Chicago while his mother worked as a dressmaker. But by 1915 he owned his own newsstand. And in 1918 he moved to Detroit to sell casualty insurance for his mother. This courageous young man would then drop out of high school to sell insurance full-time.

Within no time, Stone ran $100 into millions with his strong desire to succeed and by putting into practice the principles he educated himself on. By the time he passed on in 2002, he was not only a business mogul, but was hailed as an ‹angel› to others, lifting some from the gutter to the heights of success. When reading his works, I am fascinated by his brilliant **perspective of life. He says:** "It is interesting to note that life never leaves us stranded. If life hands us a problem, it hands us also the abilities with which to meet the problem." And I couldn't agree more.

Life has a way of sometimes handing us a raw deal. Or so it appears. We plan and dream, hope and expect but at times we end up cornered into cocoons of unintended consequences. It is possible and indeed true that we all at one point or another, have found ourselves wondering not just what's right but what's left. I believe that there is nobody that is exempted from this trial. And if it hasn't hit you, it is coming. Where everything seems lost and all hell seems to break lose. This is the point at which we feel life has stopped, we are trapped and desperately stranded.

While such a state of matters may attract a logical surrender, it behoves us to reconsider our moves beyond the immediate rationale. To be faced with despair is normal but to throw in the towel is an unwise move to make. To live to see tomorrow will constantly demand of our relentlessness in a way that ignores distress, mocks challenges and ridicules problems. The attitude that never gives up is the only thing at this point that should and must save the day. "When you get stranded, the way to start moving again is not to search for an answer but to find a new question to which your life can be the answer." (Jennifer Krause)

One question becomes immediately pertinent: 'What is it that you have in your hand." Countless times this question has been posed to you in one way or the other. It is one of the most crucial questions that we have to ask ourselves. This is not just a question but a shift of attitude, a realization of options, an exposure of secret opportunities and a confrontation of the nay-sayers propositions. Once we give an honest response to the question, we stand the chance to begin the journey of realizing that all it takes for us to move to the next level of our lives, is by using whatever we currently have available. Suddenly, what we thought was insignificant becomes sufficient and what was meagre becomes abundant enough to jumpstart a new lease of life.

This moment can become the time you realise that God does not send you into the field without equipping you with the necessary tools for the task. He has already provided you with whatever you need within you to get to that next level. If you would search within yourself you would discover the key to unlocking your desired destiny. All you need to do is look. So, what is it that you have that you excel at? What is it that you do so well that others are amazed at? Better yet, what excites you? That thing that makes you stand out among others may be what you despise most about yourself but it may be the very thing that will get you away from the rest and take you to another level.

In comparison to your need, your supply may look like a boy's lunch getting ready to be fed to five thousand men. But at least there is lunch available and that's all that's required. Miracles are the beginnings that small things need to become great things. Simply, whatever your gift is or whatever you have, work it as if lives depend on it because you know what, they do. This is the mandate that we have. To do everything in our power to move from where we are to where we ought to be. Work what you have until it begets what you want. I am persuaded that "The key to accomplishing anything in life is getting past failure." (Barbara Corcoran)

The same God that made a way in the wilderness before for you, will do it again. Don't give up, stay put. There is something in your hand that can make all the difference. Locate it and begin with it.

Motivation

Today use all the advantages you have. Add to those advantages the power of prayer. Confidence is the sure understanding that the will of God is able to empower our prayer and bring forth answers no matter the intensity, the type or the gravity of the challenge at hand. Our confidence is not in prayer itself but in the will of God to give us an advantage over every situation by answering our prayers – instantly! Today, don't pray a convenient prayer, pray according to His will! Pray in the Name of Jesus! Pray that God reveals all advantages that He has lined up in your favour! You are advantaged more than you know.

Today, walk into every room with a calculated awareness of your advantages. Recite them to yourself. Study the difference you bring. Change your life's interrogation question from 'why me?' to 'why not?' and 'what if' When eagles say: "Today we are flying high above", it is chickens that ask - 'why?' Be an eagle: don't be a chicken! Take advantage of your advantages!

Inspiration

Blessed *be* the Lord, *Who* daily loads us *with benefits*, The God of our salvation!

LESSON THIRTY

WHAT HAVE YOU BELIEVED ABOUT YOURSELF?

What we believe has a significant bearing in the development of our self confidence. The information we have interacted with over the years and the statements that have been directed at us have become the building blocks of our confidence or the lack of it. Self belief can undoubtedly be built or hindered by the feedback we receive from our environment.

On one hand, the demeaning words of parents or guardians, the intimidating utterances of insensitive spouses or lovers and the inaccurate self beliefs formed as reactions to life's experiences, can cause monumental damage to our self esteem. It can reduce our countenance into shyness, social anxiety, weak assertiveness and communication difficulties. Low self-confidence may cause us to develop a stronger than necessary critical internal voice. This tends to amplify itself we feel distressed, in moments wen we feel overwhelmed or when we feel judged by others. It is this inner critic that can cause significant personal distress by contributing to feelings of sadness, anxiety or anger, which in turn switch off our personal confidence.

Depending too much on your inner critic can kick start a concoction of unhealthy tendencies like thinking negative things about yourself, believing your negative thoughts are always true, ignoring your strengths and abilities, focusing on your mistakes and failings while ignoring your positive impacts, expecting the worst, avoiding challenges or situations where you feel you could be judged by others and thinking that you don't deserve to have pleasure or fun.

On the other hand, the lack of a deliberate life skills education makes a bad problem worse. These factors can add fuel to fire to an otherwise manageable process of human development. Lack of self confidence is a problem that doesn't have to wreck havoc; it can be thwarted.

One of the most formidable pillars of our self confidence is our belief system. Whatever we believe becomes what we naturally work to prove. If we believe we are capable, we naturally put that foot forward any time an opportunity presents itself. If we believe that we are worthless and incompetently, we shy away from challenges and opportunities.

Self-belief, otherwise referred to as self-efficacy is a person's belief in their ability to complete tasks and to achieve their set goals. Without 'belief in the ability', the ability though may be present does not find the requisite impetus to perform at optimum, or to perform at all. Self belief not only allows us the confidence to attempt new things, it also stays with us as we stay with the new thing, until we successfully finish what we start. That means that we not only begin because of our confidence but because our confidence is also the fuel for our stick-to-it-edness.

Self confidence is the ability to Judge ourselves as capable of success. And this judgement increases our chances of actual success. Judging ourselves as incapable of success reduces the chance of success. This is how critical our self belief is. It can determine if we fail or succeed in anything.

I have observed countless less qualified people, in terms of credentials; succeed more because of self confidence than those who succeed because of qualifications. I have observed people with little or no capital begin businesses with nothing but self confidence and a skill. Money doesn't need to always precede success; when we are confident of the solutions we possess, opportunities can also respond to us. Confidence is capital in itself. Self belief is leverage powerful enough to grant us equal audience at the table of greatness. If we do not have money or connections, self confidence can be the difference we bring as our offering.

How does faith affect self belief

Faith educates a deeper part of us to trust without necessarily depending on facts. Although this raises scientific questions because science is factual; faith on the other hand is not scientific.

And as much as science would want to be included in the human behavioural equation, faith has to also be included. We are realistic, but we are also intuitive.

If we always have to have facts in order to believe that we can carry out a task, then we might never get sufficient grounds to live out our dreams with full-throttle passion. Without believing that we can do it even if we do not have the experiential facts and figures of previous performance, our full potential might never have the prospect of being lived out.

Faith is very important to confidence because faith is the type of thing that builds confidence without having to justify how it did it. Faith in itself is about believing that a thing is real or true or will be real or true with no evidence that it's factually real or true while often ignoring confirmed, contradictory facts that it is not real or not true. Faith depends on truth and not on facts.

Faith is also our point of contact with divinity. Believing in God shapes what we feel capable of. This is because we now feel complemented and supported by someone better than ourselves and greater than the situation that's debasing our confidence. The feeling that God has a personal interest on us has a definite effect on our self-esteem. Without a doubt, a close personal relationship with a caring divinity is a real game changer in the equation of personal confidence.

The relationship of faith and confidence allows us to give direction to what we are confident about. Confidence does not work by itself to produce something; it works with faith. What we believe shall happen is what we confidently pursue until it happens.

Faith believes; confidence pursues.

Faith and confidence go hand in hand. In the absence of faith, it is impossible to give confidence a cause or a reason and therefore it is hard to rely on it with all our heart. Faith anchors confidence. And when our confidence is in God we make steady progress without falling prey to traps. *For the Lord becomes our confidence, and keeps our foot from being caught.*

Confidence is essentially trusting God with all our heart; leaving no options, leaning on no alternatives and letting God take the entire risk of making a way out and formulate a way forward. It is submitting all our strategies, plans and advantages to Him so they can be infused with His might as we use them. A secret ingredient of success is this: great men and women kneel down in the privacy of their personal spaces and ask for divine help. They may not publicly confess it but they do. They have this intricate thread of strength that is woven with strands of hard work, grit, dedication, courage but most importantly the prayer of faith and confidence!

The confidence of faith is about knowing that we only begin the battles which we have already won. And thus sticking to plan A and leaving the rest of the alphabet out! It is knowing that the threat exists, but it has no power to destroy us. It is encountering the devil in person, but knowing that without permission from God, he cannot touch us. It is seeing the eminent danger, the possible embarrassment and the looming gloom, but choosing to believe that only God has the final say.

Confidence is seeing ourselves in the light of God's promise in spite of the prevailing logic, storms, turbulence or uncertainty. It is sleeping through the storm while everyone else is in panic and running amok. Confidence perceives that trouble is only a custodian of our greatness and a means to an end, and not an end in itself. It knows that we don't depend on superficial, fluctuating and shaky parameters for anything, but that our confidence is anchored on the character of someone who exists beyond the limitations of men and of this world – God Himself! And that God will personally superintend over our affairs until success moves from theory to reality!

Motivation

Today, audit your faith. Do you believe that life shall work out for you? What is your faith founded on? And what do you really believe will happen in your life? Do you believe in eventual outcome of good? If you have faith, then you should have confidence. Believe that everything shall work together for your good then have confidence to create your life around that faith. Today, build your faith; then permit your confidence to function. Don't bank on the reliability of your confidence alone so you can have faith, rather, have confidence in what you have believed. Faith is dependable.

Inspiration

"Because of your little faith [your lack of trust and confidence in the power of God]; for I assure you *and* most solemnly say to you, [a]if you have [living] faith the size of a mustard seed, you will say to this mountain, 'Move from here to there,' and ... it will move; and nothing will be impossible for you."

NOTES AND REFERENCES

The Discomfort Zone
Marcia Reynolds, Psy.D.
The impostor phenomenon in high achieving women: Dynamics and therapeutic intervention - Clance, Pauline R.; Imes, Suzanne A. (1978).

Self efficacy
Albert Bandura - Bobo doll experiments and Professor Emeritus at Stanford University
What Mentally Strong People Don't Do
Amy Morin

How successful people achieve their goals
Chris Weller – Business Insider

The Psychology of Success
Joyce Marter

Coping with emotional and psychological trauma
Sidran Institute I **Authors: Lawrence Robinson, Melinda Smith, M.A., and Jeanne Segal, Ph.D.** www.helpguide.org

Leadership Strategy: Ways Body Language Impacts Leadership Results
Carol Kinsey Goman – forbes.com

Ways to Project Confidence With Your Body Language
Vivian Giang - Business Trends & Insights

You Never Get a Second Chance to Make a First Impression
Arkadin Blog Team

A Guide To Mental Preparation - believeperform.com
Gobinder Gill
Successful People Focus on the Process, not on the Result
Business Blogs - www.businessblogshub.com
Learn to focus on the process more than the results
Chomwa Shikati I medium.com
Why People Who Focus More On Processes Than Outcomes Gain More In Their Life - Casey Imafidon I www.lifehack.org

If You Want To Be Successful, Focus On The Process, Not The Outcome
Anthony Moore I www. thoughtcatalog.com
How to Become Mentally Strong
Michelle Ribeiro I www.positivepsychology.com
The springboard effect
Glen Dhliwayo I www.herald.co.zw
Religion and science: How faith can boost self-esteem
David Briggs I www.huffpost.com

What Does Confidence Have to Do With Faith?
Kenneth Copeland
The Power Of Leverage
www.digitallifementors.com
Understanding the power of leverage
www.bmmagazine.co.uk
Cognitive distortions and negative thinking
Blaz Kos
www.agileleanlife.com
When You Can't Stop Seeing the Negative in everything—Even Though You're Grateful
Margarita Tartakovsky, M.S.
www.psychcentral.com
What Is the Negativity Bias?
Kendra Cherry
www.verywellmind.com
How to take responsibility for your life: 11 no-nonsense tips
Lachlan Brown
www.hackspirit.com
KNOW YOURSELF
https://www.theschooloflife.com/thebookoflife/know-yourself/
Adam Smith
Discover Your True Self
WWW.SUCCESS.COM
The Psychology of How Well You Know Yourself
http://socialpsychonline.com/
How to deal with intimidating people
https://www.healyourpersonality.com/
Self-esteem and self-confidence
The University Of Queensland Australia - self-help resources

Printed in Great Britain
by Amazon